U.S. Department of Justice
Office of Justice Programs
National Institute of Justice

NIJ

'06

Annual Report

NATIONAL INSTITUTE OF JUSTICE

To the President, the Attorney General, and the Congress:

It is my honor to transmit the National Institute of Justice's annual report on research, development, and evaluation for fiscal year 2006, pursuant to Title I of the Omnibus Crime Control and Safe Streets Act of 1968 and Title II of the Homeland Security Act of 2002.

Respectfully submitted,

David W. Hagy
Acting Principal Deputy Director, National Institute of Justice

'06

Annual Report

NATIONAL INSTITUTE OF JUSTICE

U.S. Department of Justice
Office of Justice Programs

810 Seventh Street, N.W.
Washington, DC 20531

Michael B. Mukasey
Attorney General

Jeffrey L. Sedgwick
Acting Assistant Attorney General

David W. Hagy
Acting Principal Deputy Director, National Institute of Justice

This and other publications and products of the
National Institute of Justice can be found at:

National Institute of Justice
www.ojp.usdoj.gov/nij

Office of Justice Programs
Innovation • Partnerships • Safer Neighborhoods
www.ojp.usdoj.gov

Table of Contents

Highlights of the Year

Crime control today is a collaborative process grounded in innovative scientific research and community policing. The National Institute of Justice's (NIJ) crime and justice research evolves to meet the needs of the modern world, providing sophisticated technologies and an international perspective.

Increasing globalization and the widespread use of electronic media for communication and information exchange pose novel challenges for crime investigators. After 9/11, for example, law enforcement had to adjust and respond to the critical role of homeland security while continuing to prevent and control crime at the local level. Where electronic crimes such as cyberstalking and identity theft were rare 10 years ago, these have become prevalent and hard to target, aided by the ease of international communication and travel. Training for law enforcement now requires instruction in special investigative techniques—such as DNA analysis and computer forensics—for officers to solve and prosecute cases effectively.

NIJ provides objective, independent, evidence-based knowledge and tools to meet the challenges that crime and justice professionals face, particularly at the State and local levels. Research and development projects support the fieldwork of public safety professionals by advancing technology so that officers can make arrests without harming suspects or bystanders or endangering their own lives. Research is turned into practice that helps victims from diverse populations and communities. NIJ's partnerships with public agencies and private corporations leverage ideas and resources for use in law enforcement. Evaluations ensure return on investment and guide professionals in designing better programs. Results are published on NIJ's Web site, educating policymakers, law enforcement officers, forensic experts, scientists, electronic crime investigators, victim advocates, and criminal justice researchers.

About the National Institute of Justice

The National Institute of Justice (NIJ) is dedicated to researching, developing, and evaluating crime control and justice issues. NIJ creates resources for State and local criminal justice agencies that are relevant, timely, and cost-effective. Within the U.S. Department of Justice, NIJ is a component of the Office of Justice Programs.

In fiscal year 2006, NIJ made 514 awards for research, development, and evaluation, with an active award portfolio value of just over $1.1 billion (see appendix A).

NIJ's initiatives identify best practices; develop performance standards and conduct compliance testing for law enforcement equipment; advance law enforcement technology; improve uses of DNA and forensic evidence; increase understanding about human trafficking; and help victims of rape, assault, and domestic violence.

Challenges

Crime rates are dynamic, complex, and vary by locality. Criminologists work to understand the issues that contribute to changes that may become trends.[1] Studies suggest that social and economic conditions, incarceration rates, and law enforcement practices such as "hot spots" policing and officer account-ability may have played a role in the trends observed in the 1990s and the early 21st century.

To find the best solutions for crime control, the Nation needs NIJ to perform empirical research that combines programmatic strategies, managerial accountability, and evaluative data to understand the dynamics of crime and shape technological progress.

[1] See, for example, "Mining the Crime Drop of the 1990s for Social Clues," with A. Blumstein, J. Lauritsen, R. Rosenfeld, and F. Zimring, on National Public Radio's *Talk of the Nation Science Friday*, February 16, 2007, at www.npr.org/templates/story/story.php?storyId=7453416.

"I think that the need for empirical research on short-run change in crime at the national and local levels should be among the very highest priorities of the research community."

—Richard Rosenfeld, Ph.D., criminologist at the University of Missouri-St. Louis

Prominent results of NIJ's efforts are discussed in more detail in the following chapters. The highlights are presented here.

Faster, More Efficient Response to Crime

Technological developments are increasing communication and speeding response to crime. Several NIJ-sponsored initiatives include:

- A public-private partnership between Cisco Systems, Inc., the Danville, Virginia, Police Department, and NIJ evaluated a device that lets officers communicate instantly across State lines. The success of this initial endeavor has encouraged NIJ to launch additional partnerships involving state-of-the-art communications equipment and technologies.

- The forensic examination of electronic devices like computers, cell phones, and personal digital assistants (PDAs) has emerged as a prominent and unique field of crime investigation. In 2006, NIJ completed work on several products that enhance officers' ability to seize, extract, and store digital evidence with ease. Responding to electronic crime using digital forensics will remain a high priority at NIJ in the coming years.

- Officers have begun to use DNA analysis to investigate property crimes. An NIJ-funded study will assess how DNA can be used to solve high-volume serious crime and will identify cost-effective practices for collecting, analyzing, and using DNA evidence. Early reports indicate that DNA has helped catch burglars with extensive criminal histories. Final results of the study are expected in 2008.[2]

- Training programs on www.dna.gov, which NIJ manages, provide court and law enforcement officers with comprehensive information on how to collect forensic DNA and use DNA evidence when prosecuting a case.

Improved Safety and National Security

In 2006, NIJ continued its longstanding efforts to support law enforcement and crime and justice professionals—increasing officers' safety during pursuit and arrest, helping investigators combat terrorism and prosecute international criminals, and keeping the Nation safe from terrorist attacks.

[2] *DNA Expansion Demonstration Program*, NIJ award no. 2005–ASP–TR–015, and IAA award no(s). 2005–DN–R–095, 2005–DN–R–096, 2005–DN–R–097, 2005–DN–R–098, and 2005–DN–R–099.

- Following a rigorous evaluation, the Institute implemented new interim requirements for evaluating the performance of body armor, ensuring that manufacturers provide armor with stronger fibers that maintain their ability to stop bullets during the company's warranty period. NIJ implemented these interim requirements in 2006, certifying more than 700 models. A revised standard will be published in 2007.

- In 2006, NIJ launched a groundbreaking study to examine deaths associated with conducted-energy devices (CEDs) (also known as electromuscular disruption devices and sometimes called stun guns). The study covers the physical and psychological effects of CEDs, such as excited delirium.

- NIJ awarded several grants in fiscal year (FY) 2006 to enhance research on international terrorism. One prominent study helps courts prosecute terrorists efficiently, analyzing defense and prosecutorial strategies.[3] Another examines how Islamic militants acquire skills and practices and compares extremist networks in Spain and the United Kingdom.[4]

- NIJ began laying the groundwork to examine research strategies and frameworks needed to improve policing in a post-9/11 world.

Meeting the Needs of Victims

Research about victims and victimization in 2006 addresses the needs of diverse and international populations.

- Deaf victims and victims with limited English proficiency who experience abuse often have difficulty reporting crimes to law enforcement. NIJ provided recommendations for police training to overcome communication boundaries.

- The Prison Rape Elimination Act of 2003 (PREA) provides standards to reduce sexual assaults in prisons. NIJ issued three final reports in 2006 that directly address PREA. They discuss ways prisons can identify and counter sexual violence, systems for prisoners to report rape without social consequence, and psychological motivations behind sexual encounters in prison.

- Since 1998, NIJ has contributed knowledge to the issue of human trafficking. Research funded in 2006 will provide a comprehensive portrait of the illicit industry by which Chinese women are trafficked to other Asian

[3] *Organizational Learning and Islamic Extremism*, NIJ award no. 2006–IJ–CX–2007.

[4] *Prosecution of Terrorism Cases*, NIJ award no. 2006–IJ–CX–0026.

countries for sex work.[5] Additional projects examine the effect of antitrafficking legislation on successful prosecution.[6]

- In late 2006, NIJ considered options for building a national database of missing persons—a database that will match records of missing persons in one database with records of unidentified dead in another.

Seeking Excellence

In 2006, NIJ asked the National Academy of Sciences to perform an evaluation of NIJ's goals and operations. The evaluation will be similar to the one the Academies conducted in 1976, which prompted several revisions in NIJ's policies and program areas. The results of the new evaluation are expected to expand and sharpen NIJ's capacity to respond to crime and improve the criminal justice system.

[5] *Case Study of Human Trafficking: The Transnational Movement of Chinese Women for Sex Work,* NIJ award no. 2006–IJ–CX–0008.

[6] *Prosecuting Human Trafficking Cases: Lessons Learned and Best Practices from the U.S. and Abroad,* NIJ award no. 2006–IJ–CX–0010.

Enhancing Policing Through Science

NIJ's science efforts focus on providing criminal justice practitioners with improved tools and technologies to combat all types of crime.

Examining Less-Lethal Alternatives

New less-lethal devices expand the range at which weapons and projectiles are effective; allow officers to make a quick, harmless arrest; and advance technological standards. NIJ collaborates with the U.S. Departments of Defense, State, Energy, and Homeland Security to carry out joint projects and convert military technology for use in law enforcement.

NIJ's less-lethal portfolio suggests model policies for introducing and using less-lethal weaponry to increase its effectiveness and to reduce the possibility of injury from its use. Despite their name, less-lethal devices can be lethal when used improperly. To counter the improper use of these technologies, NIJ sponsors officer trainings, advises law enforcement, and helps agencies network with one another. For example, NIJ has collaborated with the International Association of Chiefs of Police to publish a guidance document for the use of conducted-energy devices (CEDs), which are designed to shock and incapacitate subjects without killing them.[1,2]

Evaluating CEDs. In response to reports that CED technologies may have resulted in deaths, NIJ commissioned a study called "In-Custody Deaths Due to Use of Conducted Energy Devices."[3]

NIJ's deputy director for science and technology and the president of the National Association of Medical Examiners cochair a steering group that will assign a panel to review the details of a number of deaths in which the use of a CED could not be ruled out as a possible cause. The panel will review autopsy reports of victims and incident data from police reports. Results are expected in 2008.

[1] Cronin, J.M., and J.A. Ederheimer, "Conducted Energy Devices: Development of Standards for Consistency and Guidance," Office of Community Oriented Policing Services and Police Executive Research Forum, November 2006, available at www.ojp.usdoj.gov/BJA/pdf/CED_Standards.pdf.

[2] The most widely used CED is manufactured by Taser International.

[3] See NIJ Study: "In-Custody Deaths Due to Use of Conducted Energy Devices," National Institute of Justice, available at www.ojp.usdoj.gov/nij/topics/technology/less-lethal/conducted-energy-devices.htm.

NIJ has made significant investments in less-lethal devices that use directed energy as an alternative to blunt trauma devices. These directed-energy devices deter individuals who attempt to commit illegal acts without causing them permanent harm.

NIJ-funded independent studies examine the physiological effects of CEDs. One such study assesses what happens when suspects who have been shocked with a CED experience "excited delirium," an undefined physiological state that occurs when a person's sympathetic nervous system is overexcited, possibly accompanied by a number of changes to the person's blood chemistry.[4] Some research proposes that the cause of death in shocked victims might be excited delirium rather than direct physical damage from the device itself.[5]

Examining blunt trauma devices. Blunt trauma less-lethal devices—i.e., kinetic-energy devices, like police batons, rubber bullets, or bean bags—are intended to dissuade people from taking illegal actions. Although these devices are much safer than firearms, people hit with blunt trauma devices experience a range of injuries. Depending on where they strike, such devices can cause minor bruising or more serious injuries, including broken bones, damage to internal organs, eye damage, and even death. In FY 2006, NIJ funded the Less-Lethal Monitoring Program to examine the harm these devices cause. Through this program, which operates in 11 cities, a doctor attends to the person hit with a less-lethal device onsite and at the hospital and reports medical data and status throughout the treatment process.[6] Results of the study are expected in late 2007.

Directed-energy devices. NIJ has made significant investments in less-lethal devices that use directed energy, emitting electromagnetic radiation in the form of radio or heat waves, as an alternative to blunt trauma devices. These directed-energy devices deter individuals who attempt to commit illegal acts without causing them permanent harm; instead they cause severe, yet transient, discomfort. One such less-lethal weapon technology was derived from a U.S. Department of Defense initiative called the Active Denial System and will be modified for use in law enforcement. The technology emits electromagnetic radiation (radiofrequency waves) penetrating less than 1/64 of an inch into a person's skin, exciting a person's nerve endings and quickly creating an intolerable level of discomfort. The sensation is similar to the feeling of sticking one's hand in an oven heated to 400 degrees Fahrenheit. Symptoms dissipate immediately when subjects move away from the energy path, and they experience no lasting health problems even if their eyes are exposed. NIJ's research is developing a working prototype of the device that an officer can carry.[7]

[4] *Injuries Produced by Law Enforcement's Use of Less-Lethal Weapons,* NIJ award no. 2006–DE–BX–K002.

[5] For a recently published study on excited delirium by Wake Forest researchers, see: Bozeman, W.P., and J.E. Winslow, "Medical Aspects of Less-Lethal Weapons," *The Internet Journal of Rescue and Disaster Medicine,* 5 (1) (2005).

[6] *Injuries Produced by Law Enforcement's Use of Less-Lethal Weapons: A Multicenter Trial,* NIJ award no. 2004–IJ–CX–K047

[7] *Solid-State Active Denial System Demonstration Program,* NIJ award no. 2004–IJ–CX–K035.

Workshop Develops Policing Research Agenda

What direction should NIJ's policing research take? Some 40 knowledgeable and experienced law enforcement professionals and academic leaders came together in 2006 to answer this question. The group identified several pressing topics, including:

- *Finding the best techniques for recruiting and retaining officers.*
- *Understanding the internal dynamics of police organizations and the impact of technology on policing.*
- *Identifying effective training for entry-level police officers and leadership training for first-line supervisors.*
- *Understanding how best to use CompStat concepts.[8]*

The group emphasized the need for a large-scale, multiyear research initiative to produce baseline data over time as a starting point for developing policing performance measures. These data could also be a platform for studies to assess the impact of policing practices and techniques and test innovative strategies.

Some important questions that emerged from the discussion include:

- *What steps need to be taken to develop performance measurement systems that assess the quality and effectiveness of agency- and individual-level policing?*
- *How, in what format, and to whom can research findings be disseminated so that the information is usable and, in the end, used by practitioners?*
- *How can more information be extracted from research to guide police officials on which strategies to pursue and how to implement them?*

Proceedings from the policing workshop are available at www.ojp.usdoj.gov/nij/ events/policing-research-workshop.

[8] CompStat is an innovative approach to reducing crime, first implemented by the New York City Police Department. Using a series of weekly strategy meetings and reports, it asks local police chiefs to develop tactics to target illegal activity, making them accountable for crime in their jurisdiction.

Ballistic-resistant body armor has saved more than 3,000 lives since the first models were tested in the field in 1975.

NIJ and the U.S. Department of Defense have also created a prototype of a device that emits energy on the visible and infrared spectrum, called a Personnel Halting and Stimulation Response (PHaSR).

Like the Active Denial System, the PHaSR causes discomfort by targeting a person's nerve endings. In the next 2 years, researchers will develop a range finder that will tune the PHaSR's optical energy to the appropriate power needed to achieve the desired deterrent effect.[9]

Body Armor Initiative

Ballistic-resistant body armor has saved more than 3,000 lives since the first models were tested in the field in 1975. In 2003, an officer in Forest Hills, Pennsylvania, sustained severe injuries when the body armor he was wearing failed to prevent penetration by a bullet it was designed to defeat. In response to the armor's failure, NIJ initiated a review to determine why the bullet was able to penetrate the armor.

Later that year, U.S. Attorney General John Ashcroft announced the U.S. Department of Justice's Body Armor Safety Initiative, directing NIJ to examine new and used Zylon®-based armor and to determine whether the certification process for ballistic-resistant armor required modification.

The examination showed that the Zylon® fibers comprising the body armor models of interest degrade over time when exposed to both moisture and light. In the Forest Hills incident, the fibers in the failed armor were 30 percent weaker than the fibers in a new armor vest. Additionally, 60 of 103 used armors containing Zylon® allowed at least 1 penetration during a 6-shot ballistic test. As a result, NIJ implemented the NIJ 2005 Interim Requirements for Bullet-Resistant Body Armor. These required ballistic-resistant body armor models to maintain their performance over the company's declared warranty period.[10]

To date, more than 700 models have been found in compliance with these interim requirements.

[9] The Air Force Research Laboratory at Kirtland Air Force Base in Albuquerque, New Mexico, was awarded $300,000 to improve on the infrared laser less-lethal device, in particular to reduce the size and weight of the first prototype that was produced in 2006. The project period is from July 24, 2006, to July 24, 2007.

[10] Tompkins, D. "Body Armor Safety Initiative: To Protect and Serve...Better," *NIJ Journal* 254 (July 2006): 2–6.

NIJ is currently in the process of revising the existing ballistic-resistant body armor standard and compliance testing program to help ensure the ongoing performance of armor as it ages.[11]

Sharing Information Electronically

Imagine an officer pulls a car over for speeding. The car's driver has an outstanding warrant in another State, but the ticketing officer has no access to this information. The driver departs with a simple traffic ticket. Recent NIJ-funded technological developments enhance the ability of officers to share information from databases in different jurisdictions so they can (1) obtain accurate and complete information about suspects, and (2) improve critical incident management. The Global Justice XML Data Model was developed for such information exchanges.

XML (eXtensible Markup Language) is a data formatting standard that enables disparate information systems or databases to communicate across agencies and jurisdictions. Because of the Global Justice XML initiative, led by the U.S. Department of Justice's Office of Justice Programs, justice-affiliated organizations are taking steps to ensure their existing data-sharing and exchange software is compliant with the Global Justice XML Data Model. This data can be easily shared and exchanged with the growing number of agencies using XML.

NIJ leads the research and development effort underlying this initiative, contributing more than $1 million in research, development, and technical assistance to the effort in 2006. NIJ delivers information technology that allows subscribers to NLETS (the international justice and public safety information sharing network) to share interstate driver's license data and helps law enforcement agencies exchange information through networks like the Automated Regional Justice Information System. NIJ also researches methods to raise the quality of the data being exchanged within these systems.[12]

Collaboration with the National Law Enforcement and Corrections Technology Center (NLECTC) has helped NIJ develop model Global Justice XML specifications called Information Exchange Package Documents. These serve as

[11] See *Body Armor Standards and Testing*, National Institute of Justice, available at www.ojp.usdoj.gov/nij/topics/protection/body_armor.htm.

[12] More information about NLETS and the Automated Regional Justice Information System can be found at www.ojp.usdoj.gov/nij/topics/information-led-policing/welcome.html and www.nlets.org.

The partnership has successfully evaluated one solution for Danville's interoperability challenges, and jurisdictions around the country will benefit from NIJ's assessment and recommendations for repeating the effort.

guidelines for information exchanges that meet specific business needs and have been widely adopted, acting as starting points for other Global Justice XML efforts.

Reading license plates. Automatic license plate reader (ALPR) systems scan license plates of cars driving past a certain point on a road or from a moving patrol vehicle, often reading plates in multiple lanes of traffic. They can identify stolen vehicles, stolen license plates, or vehicles with outstanding warrants, matching plates against FBI, State, or local databases that have been downloaded into the reader's processor. Field testing in a multijurisdictional task force in Maryland recovered 8 stolen cars, found 12 stolen plates, and made 3 arrests in a single shift.[13] The Long Beach, California, Police Department has four patrol cars outfitted with ALPR. The department has scanned 3.3 million plates in 15 months, identified 1,992 lost or stolen plates, recovered 490 stolen vehicles, and arrested 92 suspects.[14] Future research will develop standards for sharing database information; explore data-mining strategies for information-led policing; and evaluate policies, performance, and new plate-reading algorithms.

Public-private partnerships. The police departments in Danville, Virginia, and its neighboring counties had no way to communicate with police officers in surrounding States or counties. A major thoroughfare took suspects across county and State borders. The police could only use a cell phone to call a dispatcher, who would call a dispatcher in the neighboring county, who would call a patrol car. The system was inefficient, often resulting in missed opportunities for arrest.

When Cisco Systems, Inc., announced its Voice over Internet Protocol (VoIP) system, which would allow officers in different jurisdictions to communicate in "real time" from their patrol cars, NIJ's communications technology program, CommTech, offered to evaluate the product for the Danville Police Department. CommTech, via NLECTC, is partnering with the Danville Police Department as an honest broker and third-party evaluator.[15]

Within the partnership, Cisco provides the Danville Police Department with a VoIP system, giving the department advanced technology it might not otherwise be able to afford and allowing NIJ to independently evaluate the technology.

[13] NLECTC, "No License to Steal," *TechBeat*, Spring 2006, available at www.justnet.org/techbeat/spring2006/NoLicenseToSteal.pdf.

[14] Christopher Morgan, Long Beach Police Department, Detective Sergeant and ALPR Administrator, presentation at NIJ's Applied Technology Conference, April 3–5, 2007.

[15] The CommTech program through the NLECTC system is delivering specialized technology assistance in cutting-edge technologies.

NIJ's evaluation allows public safety agencies to understand the product's strengths and weaknesses. The partnership has successfully evaluated one solution for Danville's interoperability challenges, and jurisdictions around the country will benefit from NIJ's assessment and recommendations for repeating the effort.

The Danville pilot partnership has grown to include surrounding counties, the Commonwealth of Virginia, and the State of North Carolina.

NIJ has plans to form additional public-private partnerships to assess additional state-of-the-art technologies that may advance communications, sensor surveillance, and information-sharing for law enforcement.[16]

[16] For more information, see *Communications Technologies (CommTech),* National Institute of Justice, available at www.ojp.usdoj.gov/nij/topics/technology/communication/welcome.htm.

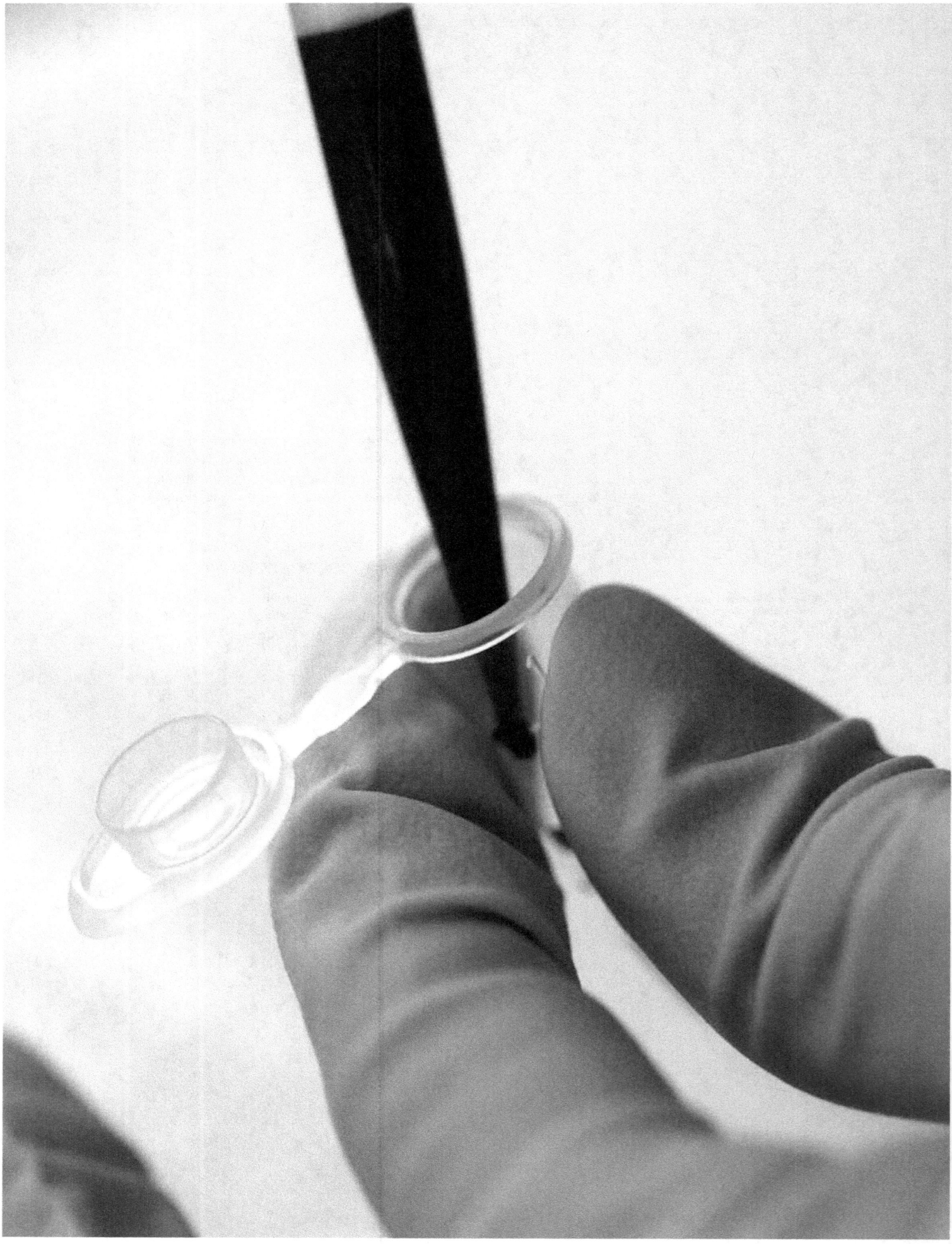

Forensic Sciences: DNA and Beyond

From the crime scene to the courtroom, forensic science plays a vital role in the criminal justice system. NIJ's investigative and forensic sciences program is dedicated to solving crime, protecting the innocent, and identifying missing persons. NIJ develops tools, technologies, products, and services that help forensic laboratories reduce their case backlogs and strengthen their capacity and capabilities.

In 2006, NIJ's forensic science portfolio included projects that advance science and technology in the following areas: [1,2]

- Anthropology.
- Controlled substances.
- Crime scene investigation.
- DNA.
- Entomology.
- Explosives detection.
- Fingerprints.
- Firearms and toolmarks.
- Impression evidence, such as shoe and tire prints.
- Pathology.
- Toxicology.
- Trace evidence, such as fibers, glass, and paint.

In addition to research and development efforts, NIJ initiated several evaluation studies to assess the impact of forensic science in identifying suspects—whether it influences a suspect's decision to confess, and whether jurors are more likely to convict suspects in cases where DNA evidence is presented. NIJ is also evaluating how controlled substances evidence affects prosecution, suspect confessions, and juror decisions.

[1] NIJ-supported research in 2006 also developed two fast-capture fingerprint prototypes and provided guidance to top-level policymakers on other biometric technologies. See the "Biometrics" chapter for further information.

[2] For information on digital evidence and electronic forensics, see the chapter "Solving Digital and Electronic Crime."

NIJ's DNA research is some of the most visible and exciting. In 2006, NIJ provided funding under the President's DNA Initiative to ensure that forensic DNA reaches its full potential to solve crimes, protect the innocent, and identify missing persons.

NIJ's DNA Vision

Through NIJ's "DNA vision," DNA will become a routine investigative tool that will enable law enforcement to focus its resources on the guilty early in an investigation and eliminate the innocent before charges are filed. NIJ will accomplish this by providing resources to State and local forensic laboratories to eliminate the current—and growing—backlog of untested evidence, to perform DNA testing in cases in which a person may have been wrongly convicted, and to identify missing persons. All the while, NIJ is committed to creating a Federal "exit strategy" to keep State and local partners on top of developments in DNA and forensics.

Significant work remains. NIJ continues to seek novel ways to improve scientists' ability to obtain DNA profiles from biological material, especially when that material is damaged or limited in quantity, by supporting a host of innovative research projects in human genetics, molecular biology, and biotechnology. In 2006, research at Ohio University and the National Institute of Standards and Technology led to a product that can generate a DNA profile from aged, degraded, or damaged samples. Known as "mini-STR," this cutting-edge DNA technology is now commercially available for identifying severely degraded human remains—often encountered in missing persons cases or mass disasters.[3]

DNA: The Ultimate Tool

Although NIJ funding supports a wide range of forensic disciplines, NIJ's DNA research is some of the most visible and exciting. In 2006, the Institute provided more than $107 million in funding under the President's DNA Initiative, a 5-year plan to ensure that forensic DNA reaches its full potential to solve crimes, protect the innocent, and identify missing persons. Information on all of NIJ's work through the President's DNA Initiative is available at www.dna.gov. In 2006, this NIJ-managed Web site was named a finalist for the Federal Web Managers Best Practice award.

[3] STR stands for short tandem repeat. STRs are short sequences of DNA repeated throughout a person's genome. They are often used in forensics to identify criminals or mass disaster victims.

Moving Research and Development to the Field

Backlog reduction. NIJ continued to provide funding to State and local DNA laboratories in 2006 to reduce the backlog of untested DNA evidence that overwhelms the Nation's crime laboratories. In 2003, officials estimated a backlog of 350,000 rape and homicide cases. To date, NIJ has provided more than $100 million to perform DNA analysis on samples in more than 60,000 cases, including approximately $4 million allocated to postconviction DNA testing. In addition, more than $100 million has been provided to enhance the capacities and capabilities of State and local laboratories.[4] As an example of the impact of NIJ's efforts in this area, during 2006, a DNA match led to the arrest of a Missouri man accused of raping a 15-year-old girl in 1997.[5]

Paul Coverdell Forensic Science Improvement Grants Program. NIJ also provided more than $18 million in assistance to State and local crime laboratories and medical examiners in 2006 under the Paul Coverdell Forensic Science Improvement Grants Program.[6] NIJ remains committed to improving the infrastructure of crime laboratories and ensuring that all forensic evidence can be analyzed in an effective, reliable, and timely manner.

GPA program. NIJ initiated the Grant Progress Assessment (GPA) program in 2005 to monitor the accountability of funding under the President's DNA Initiative.[7] In 2006, NIJ completed site visits to every State and local DNA grantee. These site visits verified that the objectives of the laboratory capacity-building and DNA backlog reduction programs are being met. NIJ also began a similar grant progress assessment for every Coverdell grantee. The GPA program will enable NIJ to strengthen its grants management and to identify model programs and promising innovations that can be shared with crime laboratories around the country.

NEST project. The NIJ Expert System Testbed (NEST) project, an evaluation of software that automates the assessment of DNA data and facilitates the entry of DNA profiles into the Combined DNA Index System (CODIS), the national DNA database, progressed tremendously in 2006.[8] This project will increase a laboratory's capacity to perform DNA analysis, thereby increasing the crime-solving potential of the national DNA database.

[4] "Forensic Casework DNA Backlog Reduction Program Formula Grants," *NIJ Awards in FY 2006*, National Institute of Justice, available at www.ojp.usdoj.gov/nij/awards/2006_topic.htm#forensic-casework.

[5] Columbia Daily Tribune staff, "DNA Leads to Arrest in 1997 Rape: 15-year-old Girl Assaulted in Her Bedroom," *Columbia Daily Tribune*, (November 8, 2006) available at www.columbiatribune.com/2006/Nov/20061108News001.asp.

[6] "Paul Coverdell Forensic Science Improvement Grants," *NIJ Awards in FY 2006*, National Institute of Justice, available at www.ojp.usdoj.gov/nij/awards/2006_topic.htm#paul-coverdell.

[7] For more information, see *Grant Progress Assessments*, National Forensic Science Technology Center, available at www.nfstc.org/programs/assessments/gpa_dna.htm.

[8] For more information, see *NIJ Expert Systems Testbed Project*, National Institute of Justice, available at www.dna.gov/lab_services/expert_systems.

Solving Cold Cases

In 1984, the decomposed remains of a person were found in a shallow grave near Deer Creek, Montana. The "Debbie Deer Creek" case was unsolved until the NIJ-supported efforts of the Center for Human Identification at the University of North Texas used mini-STR technology to positively identify Marci Bachmann, a young woman who had been missing for 22 years.

"In some of the most heartbreaking and horrendous cases, we used to have to accept that some DNA samples simply could not be tested," said Dr. Arthur Eisenberg, director of the Center. Eisenberg said that with the commercial availability of this new technology in 2006, more human remains will be identified (the most recent estimate of the number of unidentified human remains in the country exceeds 40,000) and more crimes will be solved.

The Center for Human Identification provides DNA testing of unidentified human remains and family reference samples. NIJ supports the Center's use of mini-STR technology and the development of better extraction procedures for obtaining nuclear and mitochondrial DNA (mtDNA). This work may play a critical role in advancing the Nation's ability to solve crimes, administer justice fairly, and identify remains.[9]

Training and Technology Transfer to the Field

To ensure that the results of its research and development reach as many criminal justice professionals as possible, NIJ hosts conferences, creates training tools, and publishes information on new technologies and practices. In 2006, NIJ's work developing cutting-edge tools and providing innovative forensic research reached:

- **Crime laboratory personnel** through "DNA academies" and technology transfer workshops.

[9] For more information, see Ritter, N., "Missing Persons and Unidentified Remains: The Nation's Silent Mass Disaster," *NIJ Journal* 256 (January 2007): 2–7.

To ensure that the results of its research and development reach as many criminal justice professionals as possible, NIJ hosts conferences, creates training tools, and publishes information on new technologies and practices.

- **Investigators, top-level policymakers, victim advocates, and families** through four regional conferences that focused on solving missing persons and unsolved cold cases.

- **Judges, prosecutors, and defense attorneys** through *Principles of DNA for Officers of the Court,* online training on how DNA evidence is used from the crime scene to the laboratory, and from the courtroom to postconviction testing.[10]

On the fifth anniversary of the 9/11 terrorist attacks, NIJ published a report that highlighted the use of new DNA technologies to identify severely fragmented and degraded human remains. NIJ widely disseminated *Lessons Learned From 9/11: DNA Identification in Mass Fatality Incidents* in print, electronic, and CD-ROM formats.[11] The response—nationally and internationally—has been enormous. In 2007, the report was given the first place Blue Pencil Award for Technical and Statistical Reports by the National Association of Government Communicators.

Targeting drug manufacturers. State and local law enforcement partners face challenges when targeting the continuously changing methods of meth-amphetamine manufacture. These changes make it very difficult for police to know what to look for and how to test for this illicit drug. To meet the challenge, NIJ supports the Washington State Patrol's work on identifying characteristics of emerging methamphetamine substances and manufacturing methods. NIJ also sponsors the Forensic Resource Network's training of law enforcement personnel.

Where to Go From Here: Needs Assessment

In 2006, Congress asked NIJ to assess the needs of the forensic science commu-nity. To fulfill this request, NIJ asked the National Academy of Sciences (NAS) to analyze gaps in forensic science training, equipment, space, and research. NIJ will continue to monitor NAS progress in assessing how to:

- Maximize forensic science technologies and techniques.
- Identify potential scientific advancements to assist law enforcement.
- Disseminate best practices for collecting and analyzing forensic evidence.
- Examine the role of the forensic science community in homeland security.
- Increase the number of forensic scientists and medical examiners.

[10] This training has been so successful that after an initial printing of 18,000 CD-ROMs in February 2006, NIJ printed 10,000 more in November.

[11] Kinship and Data Analysis Panel, *Lessons Learned From 9/11: DNA Identification in Mass Fatality Incidents,* September 2006, NCJ 214781.

Solving Digital and Electronic Crime

Computer forensics is a major part of today's crime scene investigations. Suspects make calls on their cell phones, record dates in their electronic calendars, describe their exploits in e-mail or in online blogs, and meet potential victims on social networking sites (e.g., MySpace). Police officers must know how to collect forensic evidence properly and obtain electronic information quickly. For example, turning off a suspect's BlackBerry® may alter evidence the device contains. NIJ's electronic crime portfolio advances and maximizes the criminal justice system's use of these evolving new media.

Recognizing and Seizing Digital Evidence

First responders must know how to recognize and seize digital evidence at a crime scene. Potential evidence may include hardware, software, storage media, wireless networking routers, CDs, thumb drives, and cell phones or personal digital assistants (PDAs). These devices can carry vital information about victims and offenders that can aid in prosecutions and missing persons cases.

NIJ's Electronic Crime Partnership Initiative (ECPI) has created a training program called *Digital Evidence Recognition for First Responders*. The program will help law enforcement officers understand the crimes in which electronically stored data might be valuable evidence. Officers will learn to recognize digital evidence and to properly seize, handle, transport, secure, and store computers and digital media without damaging the integrity of the evidence.

Mobile device forensics. An NIJ-funded grant is developing the Forensic Card Reader, a tool that allows law enforcement officers to extract data from the memory chip(s) of cell phones. The extracted information includes the user's phone book, call logs, image files, text messages, and deleted data. A device used in conjunction with the reader, called a Cell Phone Analyzer, takes the chip's data and translates it into a printed report that officers can use in investigations.

Personal electronic devices can carry vital information about victims and offenders that can aid in prosecutions and missing persons cases.

Large-Scale Code Breaking

Sometimes law enforcement officers encounter encrypted files that they cannot open. An NIJ-funded project, the Distributed Network Attack (DNA) for Large-Scale Code Breaking, creates an online solution to this problem.

When investigating officers need to open an encrypted file—in other words, need to break a code or identify the encryption key—they use a password recovery tool to gather the first 60 bytes of digital information from the encrypted file. They then electronically submit this digital information to the DNA server. Once the DNA master computer has received the investigator's submission, it parses the information to many computers on the DNA network, each of which works to assemble a small portion of the encryption key. The DNA master computer assembles all of the pieces of the encryption key and sends the results back to the investigating officers. The investigating officers then download the encryption key and enter it into the password recovery tool, enabling them to decrypt the contents of the suspect file.[1]

Distributed Network Attack Code-Breaking System Process

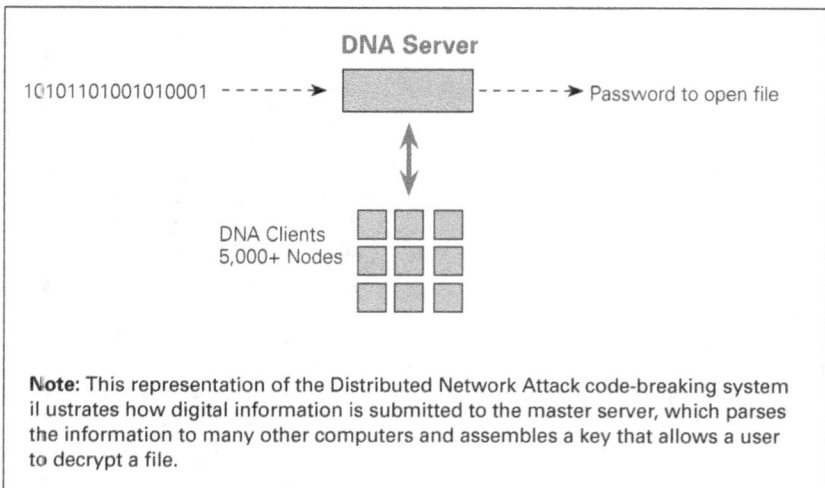

Note: This representation of the Distributed Network Attack code-breaking system illustrates how digital information is submitted to the master server, which parses the information to many other computers and assembles a key that allows a user to decrypt a file.

[1] *Distributed Network Technology for Large-Scale Code Breaking (The DNA Project),* NIJ award no. 2005–DE–BX–K034.

Computer Forensics Tool Testing Project

NIJ collaborates with the National Institute for Standards and Technology (NIST) through a program called the Computer Forensics Tool Testing (CFTT) project. CFTT tests the digital evidence acquisition and analysis tools that investigators use to determine whether tools work as they should.[2]

In FY 2006, the project tested a number of write block devices, which preserve the integrity of digital evidence when officers remove data from an electronic device. Thirteen test results were published in 2006 and are available through the NIJ and NIST Web sites.[3]

Experts Guide NIJ's E-Crime Efforts

The NIJ-funded Electronic Crime Partnership Initiative (ECPI) finds technology solutions for State and local law enforcement by building and sustaining partnerships with criminal justice, industry, and academia. ECPI's multidisciplinary team helps law enforcement officers solve computer crimes. For example, ECPI cosponsored a "Bag-'n'-Tag" course to teach officers how to recognize, seize, and handle digital evidence at a crime scene. In 2006, ECPI continued to explore solutions to eliminate one of the major impediments to a cybercrime prosecution: the time it takes for an Internet service provider (ISP) to respond to a subpoena. Currently, ISPs can take several weeks to produce records, but with the creation of secure, limited-access servers around the country, ISPs could respond more quickly to subpoenas and increase the number of successful prosecutions.[4]

[2] Learn more at NIST's site: www.cftt.nist.gov.

[3] See "Write Block Devices," *Computer Forensic Tool Testing*, National Institute of Justice, available at www.ojp.usdoj.gov/nij/topics/ecrime/cftt.htm#writeblock.

[4] For more information, see NIJ's Web site on ECPI at www.ojp.usdoj.gov/nij/topics/ecrime/ecpi.htm.

Advancing Biometric Identification

Biometrics is the automated use of biological and physical characteristics to recognize a person's identity. Faster and more accurate identification enhances officer safety, detects criminals, secures facilities and information systems from unauthorized access, makes borders more secure, and prevents identity theft.

Setting the National Agenda on Biometrics

The Executive Office of the President of the United States organized the National Science and Technology Council's Subcommittee on Biometrics to shape national efforts and coordinate Federal agencies with an interest in biometrics. The subcommittee is dedicated to finding the best ways to achieve real-time identification and tracking and to increase personal, corporate, and government security.

The biometrics subcommittee, cochaired by an NIJ senior program manager, is a collaborative team of 13 government organizations that creates White House–level policies on the development and use of biometrics. In 2006, the subcommittee produced 14 documents that educate program managers, law enforcement, and the general criminal justice audience on the latest advances in biometric technology.[1] Producing these documents laid the groundwork for the subcommittee's future projects. Upcoming initiatives involve investing in projects that advance biometric technologies; protect privacy; and strengthen interagency, international, and public-sector partnerships.

The subcommittee will also facilitate an informed debate on biometrics and privacy. The debate is expected to spur discussion about the ethics involved in using these technologies and how they can be most effective.[2]

[1] The documents include a biometrics glossary; an FAQ; guides to biometric technologies; and a report on methods used in face, hand, fingerprint, and speaker recognition. They are available at www.biometrics.gov.

[2] See Blackburn, D., "Taking Today's Biometrics to Meet Tomorrow's Needs: Meeting the Challenge Together," PowerPoint Presentation, NSTC Subcommittee on Biometrics, September 2006, available at www.biometrics.gov/NSTC/BCC2006.pdf.

"If successful, the fingerprint initiative will leave a valuable legacy for law enforcement."

—James B. Comey, Former Deputy Attorney General

Fast-Capture Initiative

Standard fingerprinting techniques require an officer to grasp an individual's hand and roll each of his fingers across a fingerprint card or live-capture scanner. The technique takes several minutes, requires a trained technician, and does not capture an imprint of the side of the hand or the palm—parts of the hand investigators often collect prints from at crime scenes.

NIJ-funded scientists and engineers are working on new tools and techniques that will capture the equivalent of 10 rolled fingerprints in less than 15 seconds and both palm prints in less than 1 minute. NIJ's fast-capture initiative will improve fingerprint image quality, decrease the time it takes to capture fingerprints, and develop products that are affordable and can be manufactured in the near future.

NIJ collaborates with several agencies on the fingerprint initiative—the Defense Advanced Research Projects Agency, the Federal Bureau of Investigation, the U.S. Department of Homeland Security, and the Justice Management Division. Between 2005 and 2007, this initiative will give more than $8.3 million to fund four projects at universities and corporations across the Nation.[3]

Three unique technological approaches are being used to find a fast-capture fingerprinting technology:

- Two projects use high-resolution camera imaging to capture fingerprints. One such model, created by Carnegie Mellon University, constructs a three-dimensional visual model of the entire hand using 10 micro-cameras positioned at different angles to image the hand.[4]

- A project by TBS North America, Inc., uses a three-camera system that captures the print as it scans under the fingers. The system captures detailed finger ridge and valley characteristics using novel image-processing algorithms.[5]

- A project by Cross Match Technologies, Inc., uses a two-dimensional silicon contact sensor array on a polymer plastic foil to capture an equivalent rolled fingerprint. The polymer conforms to the shape of the finger on contact. A 64 x 64–pixel model has been developed and tested.[6]

These projects produced two single-finger prototypes in 2006, which experts at NIJ and the National Institute of Standards and Technology reviewed and approved for further development. Future prototypes will capture all fingers or the entire hand; final prototypes are anticipated in 2007 and 2008.

[3] Miles, C., *Sensors and Surveillance (SSU) Program Plan,* PowerPoint presentation, National Institute of Justice, January 2007.

[4] *Handshot ID: A Fast 3–D Imaging System for Capturing Fingerprints, Palm Prints, and Hand Geometry,* NIJ award no. 2005–IJ–CX–K060.

[5] *Fast Capture Technology to Capture Up to 10 Roll-Equivalent Fingerprints Within 15 Seconds,* NIJ award no. 2005–IJ–CX–K071.

[6] *Fast Capture Fingerprint and Palm Print Technology,* NIJ award no. 2005–IJ–CS–K067.

Mobile Biometrics

In 1999, NIJ funded the development of the Integrated Biometric Identification System (IBIS), a device that allowed patrol officers to capture facial images and fingerprints and checked them against the local identification system. The device was large, weighed 5 pounds, cost $6,000, and returned search results in 2 to 3 minutes.

In 2006, technological advances led to the introduction of the BlueCheck™ device, which is smaller than a cell phone, weighs 3 ounces, costs $1,500, and returns a fingerprint search in less than 1 minute. The device uses Bluetooth® technology to send fingerprint data to the computer in the officer's patrol car. The San Joaquin County, California, Sheriff's Department began testing the device in 2006. Within a week, they arrested more than 12 parolees with outstanding warrants.[7]

The Pinellas County Sheriff's Office in Florida has been using digital cameras to take facial mugshots of suspects in the field. Over the past 2 years, deputies in Pinellas County have used these cameras to correctly identify 295 people who lied about their identity. There are currently 50 Pinellas County Sheriff's Office patrol cars equipped with mobile facial recognition technology.[8]

NIJ has provided funds for a number of police departments across the country to buy and test these products. Their success has inspired a number of companies to begin manufacturing and selling similar mobile fingerprinting devices.

Facial Identification

Facial recognition technologies hold the potential to increase security and officer safety by identifying suspects. These recognition systems use advanced, multidimensional imaging techniques to piece together facial images. In 2006, an NIJ-funded project at Sonic Foundry, Inc., produced a prototype of facial recognition and audio analysis software.[9]

Other facial recognition systems funded in 2006 continue to advance the technologies involved in suspect identification. A grant at the New Jersey Institute of Technology is developing a system that uses an advanced algorithm to identify faces.[10] This algorithm has shown success in solving other complex

[7] Television news reports describing the BlueCheck™ device in San Joaquin County, California, can be found at www.news10.net/display_story.aspx?storyid=24024, and cbs13.com/local/local_story_031192349.html.

[8] "Mobile Facial Recognition Technology Used To Identify Wanted Suspect Who Fled From Deputies After Suspicious Incident," Press Release, Pinellas County Sheriff's Office, August 23, 2006, available at pcsoweb.com/News%20Releases/ReleaseItem.aspx?id=1018.

[9] Advanced Media Analysis Project, NIJ award no. 2003–IJ–CX–K001.

[10] Facial and Iris-Based Biometric System, NIJ award no. 2006–IJ–CX–K033.

pattern-recognition problems. Another grant, awarded to GE Global Research Corporation, will create a prototype of a program that extracts facial images from surveillance video. The images are rotated in three dimensions as necessary and combined to produce a recognizable image.[11]

Iris Recognition

Each person has a unique iris that can be used for individual identification. Iris-recognition systems take a picture of an individual's eyes and scan a computer system for a match. The picture acts as a personal ID that can grant access to office buildings, accounts, or other limited-access entities.

One of NIJ's biometric projects involved piloting a program to use iris recognition to guarantee children's safety. Following successful pilot testing in the New Egypt, New Jersey, school system in 2003, a second round of iris-recognition prototype systems was installed in the Freehold Borough, New Jersey, school district in FY 2006.[12] This system improved on the New Egypt system by adding automatically printed badges and "tailgating" technology, a way to make sure someone cannot hold a door open for others to enter. Researchers also improved the locations of the iris systems to increase their accuracy.

Setting Standards for Face and Iris Recognition Technology

In partnership with the National Institute of Standards and Technology, NIJ sponsored two "technology potlucks" in 2006. Thirty domestic and international organizations came together to evaluate and test state-of-the-art face- and iris-recognition technologies at the "Face Recognition Vendor Test" and "Iris Challenge Evaluation." The vendors brought their refined algorithms or software programs to help scientists determine which algorithms were most effective at matching faces or irises.[13]

Learn more about the Face Recognition Vendor Test at face.nist.gov/frvt/frvt2006/frvt2006.htm and the Iris Challenge Evaluation at iris.nist.gov/ice.

[11] *Active 3-D Face Capture,* NIJ award no. 2006–IJ–CX–K045.

[12] Cohn, J.P., "Keeping an Eye on School Security: The Iris Recognition Project in New Jersey Schools," *NIJ Journal* 254 (July 2006): 12–15.

[13] An algorithm is a step-by-step computational procedure for solving a problem in a finite number of steps.

Biometrics Online

NIJ cosponsors some of the top Web sites for biometrics information. Biometrics.gov (www.biometrics.gov) is the central source of information on biometrics-related activities of the Federal Government. Two sister sites— www.biometricscatalog.org and www.biometrics.org—provide a repository of biometrics-related public information and opportunities for discussion.

These sites encourage greater collaboration and information sharing in the field of biometrics research, providing current, free information to the crime and justice community and the general public.

Victims and Victimization

NIJ's Violence Against Women and Family Violence research program works to respond effectively to the needs of women and families who face abuse and victimization and to expand the criminal justice system's capacity to respond to an increasingly diverse population.

In FY 2006, NIJ expanded this research program's focus on violence against women with diverse language skills, physical abilities, resources, and cultural backgrounds. Although communities face challenges when responding to physical or sexual abuse, the linguistic or cultural barriers faced by certain communities may further hamper the criminal justice system's response to such crimes.

NIJ awarded $5.2 million to study violence and victimization in FY 2006; much of the funding was made possible by the Violence Against Women Act of 2005. NIJ managed 17 active grants during that time related to domestic violence, sexual violence, and elder abuse.[1]

In creating initiatives to target violence against women, NIJ collaborates with the U.S. Department of Justice's Office on Violence Against Women and Office for Victims of Crime. These partnerships flourished in 2006, as did those with the U.S. Departments of Defense, Education, and Health and Human Services. Joint activities maximize Federal efforts to share ideas, disseminate findings, and identify ways to address domestic violence, sexual assault, teen dating violence, and stalking.

Domestic Violence

Statistics show that 22.1 percent of women experience intimate partner violence, in comparison with 7.4 percent of men in their lifetime.[2] NIJ's domestic violence portfolio focuses on understanding the extent of violence against women and family members, identifying the causes and correlates of violence, and evaluating interventions. Research in 2006 has taken steps to improve judges' ability to meet the needs of battered immigrant women and to find innovative ways to monitor and modify batterer behavior.[3]

[1] For complete information about NIJ's violence against women portfolio, see the compendium of grants at www.ojp.usdoj.gov/nij/vawprog/vaw_portfolio.pdf.

[2] Tjaden, P., and N. Thoennes, *Full Report of the Prevalence, Incidence, and Consequences of Violence Against Women: Findings From the National Violence Against Women Survey,* November 2000, NCJ 183781; and Tjaden, P., and N. Thoennes, *Extent, Nature, and Consequences of Rape Victimization: Findings From the National Violence Against Women Survey,* January 2006, NCJ 210346.

[3] For example, a grant awarded to the BOTEC Analysis Corporation is examining the use of polygraph technology to monitor probation violations among high-risk batterers in the community: *Use of Polygraphs to Combat Violence Against Women,* NIJ award no. 2005–WG–BX–0010.

As a way of meeting the needs of those who have been abused or neglected, NIJ sponsors workshops that bring together practitioners from the field, subject-matter experts, and policymakers to learn from one another and help shape the agency's research agenda.

Gathering Input From the Field

As a way of meeting the needs of those who have been abused or neglected, NIJ sponsors workshops that bring together practitioners from the field, subject-matter experts, and policymakers to learn from one another and help shape the agency's research agenda.

In 2006, NIJ sponsored two of these workshops. A workshop held in August on violence against women was designed to coordinate Federal efforts in the field. Federal professionals discussed strategies for disseminating information, improving methodology and study design, creating effective support systems, and initiating research where subject-matter experts still have questions.

Another workshop, in June, highlighted the importance of combating teen dating violence, bringing together 17 field experts to craft and enrich future research and discuss current programs to address the problem. The extent of teen victimization is difficult to estimate because adolescents are often unwilling to report violence. In a recent Centers for Disease Control and Prevention study, about 9 percent of high school students reported that violence occurred in their relationships.[4] Recent initiatives, since the passing of the Violence Against Women Act of 2005, have strengthened efforts and strategies to target this type of abuse.

Proceedings from these workshops are available at www.ojp.usdoj.gov/nij/ vawprog/conferences.html.

---

[4] Centers for Disease Control and Prevention, "Physical Dating Violence Among High School Students—United States," *Morbidity and Mortality Weekly Report* 55 (19) (2003): 529–552.

[5] Uekert, B.K., T. Peters, W. Romberger, M. Abraham, and S. Keilitz, *Servicing Limited English Proficient (LEP) Battered Women: A National Survey of the Courts Capacity to Provide Protection Orders,* October 2006, NCJ 216072.

Victims who speak limited English. NIJ-funded researchers investigated judges' ability to meet the needs of battered women with limited English proficiency.[5] The findings suggest that judges perceive they are meeting victims' needs, but the victims often do not feel their needs are met. Many courts provided an interpreter only at the final stage of a protection order, and smaller courts often could not find qualified interpreters. The study's

Does Juvenile Delinquency Lead to Adult Criminal Behavior?

Research has shown a connection between juvenile delinquency in boys and later adult crime. Similar research on juvenile delinquent girls—a growing segment of the juvenile justice population—has not been conducted. In 2006, NIJ funded a study that will examine whether female juvenile delinquents become adult criminals, and whether men and women who were incarcerated as juveniles are more likely to abuse or neglect their children. The study will follow a sample of 1,000 formerly incarcerated juvenile delinquents from the date of their release to their 28th birthdays.[6]

recommendations include providing forms in multiple languages, improving outreach, and advancing language and interpretation services.

Victims from other countries. An NIJ grant awarded to the University of Minnesota will examine the victimization and legal problems experienced by battered women who were charged with international child abduction under the Hague Convention after they fled to the United States to escape abusive partners.[7]

Sexual Violence

The National Violence Against Women Survey, sponsored by NIJ and the Centers for Disease Control and Prevention (CDC), estimates that more than 300,000 women and 93,000 men are raped each year.[8] To improve the criminal justice system's response to sexual assault and rape, NIJ's sexual violence portfolio has researched the nature and prevalence of these crimes and the efficacy of interventions. NIJ evaluates the multisystem response to sexual violence and the use of forensic approaches to sexual assault cases. The research program also emphasizes the importance of examining sexual violence as it occurs in diverse communities.

Victims in the deaf community. Research has shown that women who have been sexually assaulted are unlikely to report their victimization to the police.

[6] *Long-Term Consequences of Delinquency: Child Mal-treatment and Crime in Early Adulthood,* NIJ award no. 2006–IJ–CX–0014.

[7] *Justice System Response to Intimate Partner Violence,* NIJ award no. 2006–WG–BX–0006.

[8] Tjaden and Thoennes, 2006.

Women who are deaf or hard of hearing often have particular difficulty reporting sexual assault to law enforcement officials and receiving services. An NIJ-funded study examined how service providers and law enforcement can identify and meet the needs of women in the deaf community who have been sexually assaulted.[9] Findings show deaf women's experiences reporting encounters to the police were often frustrating because police frequently refused to write notes to communicate and had limited knowledge of sign language. Police stations were often inadequately equipped to respond to deaf sexual assault victims, lacking such services as around-the-clock sign language interpreters. The study suggests that police and service providers need additional education and training programs.

Victims who are revictimized. An NIJ-funded study examined the sexual assault histories of women and how these histories may have led to their incarceration or affected their current mental and physical health. The Kansas-based study gathered data about women living in a rural community, women receiving social services, and women being incarcerated. It examined whether past victimization could influence women's propensity to violence.[10] Of the 423 women in the study, 85 percent reported being sexually assaulted, with the highest percentage in the prison community. More than 90 percent of the women had experienced intimate partner violence. Experiencing physical and sexual abuse as a child had a negative impact on a woman's physical and mental health as an adult. Rape in adulthood had a negative impact on women's physical and mental health, but intimate partner violence in adulthood did not appear to affect women's well-being. The authors suggest that early intervention and social services for assault victims can prevent criminal behavior in adulthood.

Elder Abuse

The best available estimates state that between 1 and 2 million Americans over the age of 65 have been "injured, exploited, or otherwise mistreated by someone on whom they depended for care or protection."[11] Elderly people who are physically abused or neglected often have few support structures for reporting the abuse, and the criminal justice system does not often prosecute the abusers. NIJ supports the development of new measurements of elder

[9] Obinna, J., S. Krueger, C. Osterbaan, J.M. Sadusky, and W. DeVore, *Understanding the Needs of Victims of Sexual Assault in the Deaf Community,* February 2006, NCJ 212867.

[10] Postmus, J.L., and M. Severson. *Violence and Victimization: Exploring Women's Histories of Survival,* November 2005, NCJ 214440.

[11] Bonnie, R.J., and R.B. Wallace, eds., *Elder Mistreatment: Abuse, Neglect, and Exploitation in an Aging America,* Washington, DC: National Academies Press, 2002.

abuse and neglect, gathering more accurate incidence and prevalence data to inform policy and practice. In addition, NIJ-funded research strives to develop forensic markers of elder abuse to detect this underreported crime. One FY 2006 study at the University of California examines pressure ulcers in the elderly and will determine when an ulcer is a sign that that person has been abused.[12]

Preventing Child and Family Violence

Innovative prevention programs target violent behavior at its roots, before it starts. Several NIJ evaluations funded in FY 2006 examine the effectiveness of a number of programs that strive to prevent violent behavior in children or families:

- ***Violence prevention.*** *SAFEChildren, in Illinois, targets children starting the first grade who come from high-risk, inner-city communities and tries to shape their behavior to avoid later delinquency and school failure.[13]*

- ***"Tribes" learning communities.*** *This intervention in Washington State, aimed at elementary school students, trains teachers to create a supportive learning environment that fosters benevolent relationships and behaviors.[14]*

- ***Healthy Families New York.*** *This program is intended to prevent child abuse by providing home treatment services to families where children are at risk of maltreatment. An NIJ evaluation will test how well the program prevents child abuse and neglect, changes parenting behavior, and reduces a child's propensity to delinquency.[15]*

[12] *Multisite Study to Characterize Pressure Ulcers in Long-Term Care Under Best Practices,* NIJ award no. 2006–IJ–CX–0029.

[13] *Evaluation of SAFEChildren, A Family-Focused Prevention Program,* University of Illinois, NIJ Award No. 2006–JP–FX–0062.

[14] *Outcome Evaluations of Tribes Learning Communities,* NIJ award no. 2006–JF–FX–0059.

[15] *Randomized Trial of Healthy Families New York: Does It Prevent Child Maltreatment?* NIJ award no. 2006–MU–MY–0002

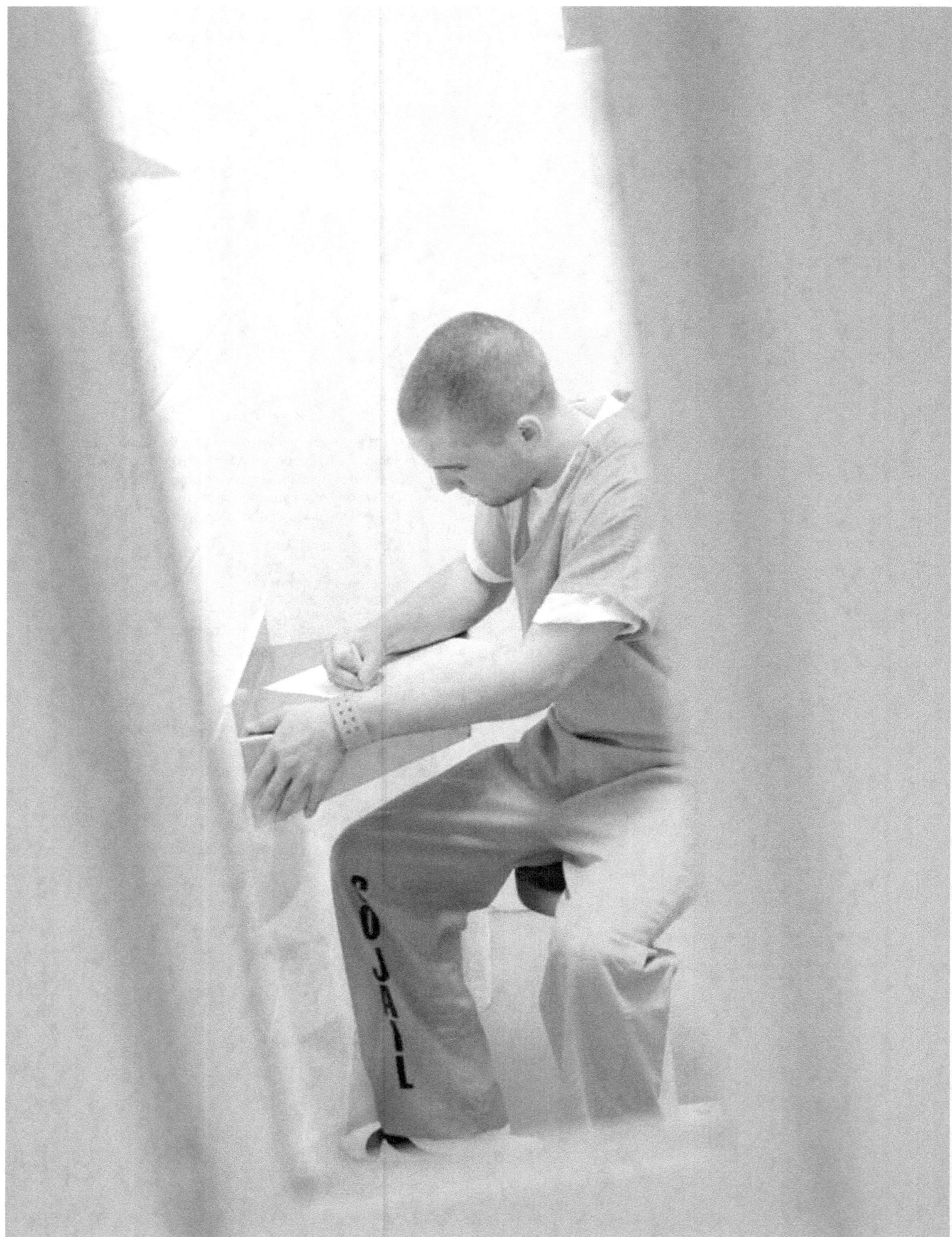

Corrections: Improving Programs and Practices

More than 7 million people—3.2 percent of all American adults—were incarcerated or on parole in 2005.[1] NIJ's corrections portfolio funds research, development, and evaluation initiatives to make prisons safer for both inmates and corrections officers, to assess alternate sentencing, and to evaluate prison reentry initiatives.

Making Prisons Safer

In 2005, approximately 6,241 prisoners, or 2.8 per 1,000, reported that they had experienced sexual violence while incarcerated. The highest number of allegations involved staff-initiated sexual misconduct against inmates, closely followed by inmate-against-inmate nonconsensual sexual acts.[2] Although this rate was an increase from 2004, the reported incidence of sexual assault in prisons is low—a recent meta-analysis suggested that only 1.91 percent of prisoners reported sexual victimization over a lifetime of incarceration.[3]

In a study that examined inmates' perceptions of prison sex and sexual violence, 33.5 percent of male and 28.2 percent of female prisoners reported they were aware of a fellow inmate who had been raped by a staff member.[4] The same study, however, also found that 28 percent of men and 32 percent of women inmates felt that the policies and procedures of the prison they lived in could protect them from rape. NIJ's research in 2006 focused on understanding the prison culture that surrounds sexual violence and finding pathways to eliminate sexual violence and penalize offenders.

Congress passed the Prison Rape Elimination Act (PREA) in 2003 to create standards to reduce sexual violence in prisons, provide accurate information about the violence that occurs in corrections facilities, and increase prison accountability for inmate safety.

[1] *Corrections Statistics*, Bureau of Justice Statistics, available at www.ojp.usdoj.gov/bjs/correct.htm.

[2] *Corrections Officials Reported More Than 6,200 Sexual Violations in the Nation's Prisons and Jails During 2005*, Bureau of Justice Statistics, available at www.ojp.usdoj.gov/bjs/pub/press/svrca05pr.htm.

[3] Gaes, G.G., and A.L. Goldberg, *Prison Rape: A Critical Review of the Literature*, March 2004, NCJ 213365.

[4] Fleisher, M.S., and J.L. Krienert, *The Culture of Prison Sexual Violence*, 2006, NCJ 216515.

Since then, NIJ has awarded eight grants to researchers investigating sexual violence in prisons. Three studies were completed in 2006 and issued final reports.

1. **Sexual violence in Texas prisons.** Texas prisons report the highest number of sexual assaults in the Nation, almost four times the national average. An NIJ-funded study assessed how the environment of the Texas prison system contributes to the high assault rate, how Texas's Safe Prison program functions to decrease assaults, and what aspects of the Texas program could be incorporated into other State models.[5]

   The study's findings suggest that prisoners in Texas report incidents at relatively low rates. Allegations are often difficult to substantiate, mostly because prisoners delay reporting incidents, making it difficult for officers to find witnesses or physical evidence. Assailants were profiled as older than the victims, more likely to be black or Hispanic, often involved in gang activity, and more likely to be involved in other criminal offenses. The report suggests ways prisons can profile victims and assailants, and recommends increased staff efforts to monitor and prevent assaults.

2. **The social structure behind violence.** A series of anonymous interviews examined inmate perceptions of prison sexual violence and how the prison community responds to incidents. Inmates described a self-policing prison system with protective social arrangements that kept many inmates safe from harm. They thought sexual violence did not occur frequently and suggested that only a victim's interpretation of an aggressive encounter could determine if it was rape. Some inmates used sex to repay debts, had sex with officers to receive contraband, or became involved in consensual homosexual encounters.

   Researchers suggested that prison staff should focus on increasing inmate supervision and finding better ways to resolve inmate concerns. Prisons need to revise their systems for examining reported incidents so that investigations support victims' needs and do not isolate them from their community.[6]

3. **Policies to counter sexual violence.** An NIJ-funded study surveyed State corrections leaders on the policies and programs they were using to address sexual violence. Researchers identified working practices and visited State sites that had promising approaches to reducing sexual violence.

[5] Austin, J., T. Fabelo, A. Gunter, and K. McGinnis, *Sexual Violence in the Texas Prison System*, 2006, NCJ 215774.

[6] Fleisher, M.S., and J.L. Krienert, *The Culture of Prison Sexual Violence*, 2006, NCJ 216515.

Through PIECP, prisoners work for private companies, earning the prevailing wage and acquiring skills they can use to secure employment postrelease. They gain work experience, support their families, save money for the future, and offset the cost of their incarceration, reimbursing the State.

Their findings suggest that prevention programs might include inmate and officer education, successful prosecution of offenders, better investigation and documentation of incidents, cooperation with outside experts and community groups, and further involvement with PREA. Prisons should focus on providing programs that support a victim's decision to report sexual offenses.[7]

Employment in Prison

Prisoners working under the supervision of corrections staff for a modest sum have been a mainstay of corrections for more than 150 years. A recent prison work program, the Prison Industry Enhancement Certification Program (PIECP) allows local corrections facilities to partner with private companies, providing inmates with jobs such as glove manufacturing, papaya packing, boat building, and car refurbishing. In 2006, NIJ reported findings from an evaluation of this program. Through PIECP, prisoners work for private companies, earning the prevailing wage and acquiring skills they can use to secure employment after their release. They gain work experience, support their families, save money for the future, and offset the cost of their incarceration, reimbursing the State.

The evaluation revealed that PIECP participants obtained employment more quickly after release and maintained it longer than those who worked in the traditional correctional industries programs and those who were involved in nonwork activities or were idle while imprisoned. For example, 55 percent of PIECP workers obtained employment within 3 months of release, compared to 40 percent of inmates in the other study groups. PIECP program participants also had lower rates of rearrest, conviction, and incarceration than participants in other prison work programs.

NIJ's evaluation also revealed that the wages earned by PIECP participants benefited taxpayers. A significant portion of PIECP participants' wages go directly to the State to cover the cost of prisoner room and board.[8]

Providing Postrelease Services

Making the transition from prison to society can be difficult for many people who are incarcerated—they must find employment and housing and often have to support their children. The Serious and Violent Offender Reentry

[7] Zweig, J.M., R.L. Naser, J. Blackmore, and M. Schaffer, *Addressing Sexual Violence in Prisons: A National Snapshot of Approaches and Highlights of Innovative Strategies*, 2007, NCJ 216586.

[8] For more information on NIJ's evaluation of the Prison Industry Enhancement Certification Program, see Smith C., J. Bechtel, A. Patrick, R.R. Smith, and L. Wilson-Gentry, *Correctional Industries Preparing Inmates for Reentry: Recidivism and Postrelease Employment*, May 2006, NCJ 214608; and Moses, M.C., and C. Smith, "Factories Behind Fences: Do Prison 'Real Work' Programs Work?" *NIJ Journal* 257 (June 2007): 32–35.

Initiative (SVORI) provides prisoners with postrelease services, helping them reenter the public community. In 2003, NIJ began a multisite evaluation of SVORI to assess the extent to which the program helps prisoners access appropriate, comprehensive, integrated services; improves prisoners' employment possibilities, health, and personal well-being; and reduces future criminal activity.

The SVORI evaluation (www.svori-evaluation.org) measures program success by examining a number of individual outcomes, such as employment, family stability, mental health, and substance abuse. Preliminary findings from 2006 indicate:

- Participants have moderately more success gaining employment and housing and meeting other measurements of success than nonparticipants.

- Participants are more likely to receive postrelease services than nonparticipants, but the overall level of service provision is low.

- Most programs have enrolled fewer people than they originally projected.

- Most programs will continue providing some services for inmates even after their funding has ended.[9]

Assessing Sentencing and Probation Policies

Recent policies in some States offer drug users alternatives to time in prison. NIJ awarded a grant in 2006 to the Vera Institute of Justice to evaluate the impact of Kansas Senate Bill 123, which provides drug abuse treatment instead of prison time to nonviolent drug possession offenders. The bill took effect in November 2003. The evaluation will measure how this program affects future drug use, recidivism, and other behaviors, comparing offenders sentenced in this manner to those sentenced to time in prison and standard probation.[10] Another 2006 evaluation assesses how probation officers' caseload size and use of evidence-based practices affect recidivism rates for medium- and high-risk probationers.[11]

[9] RTI International and Urban Institute, *Roundtable Discussion: Policy Implications of Findings from the Multi-Site Evaluation of SVORI*, International Association of Reentry Consortium, March 20, 2007.

[10] *Alternate Sentencing Policies for Drug Offenders: Evaluating the Effectiveness of Kansas Senate Bill 123*, NIJ award no. 2006–IJ–CX–0032.

[11] *Multijurisdictional Study of Reduced Caseload and Related Supervision Strategies in Managing Offenders on Probation*, NIJ award no. 2006–IJ–CX–0011.

NIJ Research Published in Corrections Today

NIJ collaborates with the American Correctional Association (ACA) to disseminate corrections-related research to the field. NIJ's column in each issue of ACA's professional membership magazine, Corrections Today, covers a range of topics. In 2006, the columns included:

February	NIJ's Response to the Prison Rape Elimination Act
April	No More Cell Phones
June	Duress Systems in Correctional Facilities
August	Brief Mental Health Screening for Corrections Intake
October	Correlating Incarcerated Mothers, Foster Care, and Mother-Child Reunification
December	No Shortcuts to Successful Reentry: The Failings of Project Greenlight

Getting the Word Out

NIJ disseminates information through a variety of outlets, helping taxpayers receive the maximum benefits of research, development, and evaluation. Communicating information on research findings and technological advancements depends on a multipronged approach to communications. Print and electronic publications and NIJ's respected conferences and training workshops lead NIJ's innovative communications strategy. Collaboration with outside communications resources, such as Harvard University, results in dual hosting of Web chats and the creation of interactive Web- and CD-based training tools.

Internet Outreach

Whether findings are published in a written report, on a CD, or another device, all of NIJ's work is available on the Web. NIJ's site, www.ojp.usdoj.gov/nij, offers easy access to NIJ-sponsored research reports, descriptions of NIJ programs, information about grant awards, and agency announcements. In FY 2006, NIJ issued 39 solicitations and made 514 awards. The Institute posted 96 final grant reports to the Web and published 65 documents and CD-ROMs.

Nearly 1.5 million people visited NIJ's Web site in 2006, an increase of more than 20 percent from 2005. All NIJ products are posted on its Web site in a format accessible to people with disabilities. NIJ continues to enhance the site's capabilities, updating search techniques and expanding subject matter. A redesigned Web site will launch in 2007.

www.dna.gov. To provide the general public with the most current information on DNA and biological forensics, NIJ manages www.dna.gov, the official Web site of the President's DNA Initiative. The site features updates on groundbreaking DNA research, how that research applies to criminal justice, and how DNA and forensics researchers can obtain grants in biological forensics.

In FY 2006, www.dna.gov published online training designed for key criminal justice practitioners, including *Principles of Forensic DNA for Officers of the*

"The training courses fulfilled a requirement for one of our General Orders on the proper collection of DNA evidence. [. . .] The interactive programming alleviated the monotony associated with other simpler read and test online courses. It was very beneficial in fulfilling our needs."

—Lt. Phil LaBenda, Administrative Division, Clayton, Missouri, Police Department

Court, to assist judges, prosecutors, and defense lawyers in using DNA evidence. The site also hosts beginning and advanced training courses for first responders, investigators, and evidence technicians, called *What Every Law Enforcement Officer Should Know About DNA Evidence.*[1] These courses have met with outstanding success; several new courses are being developed.

www.ncjrs.gov. NIJ cosponsors the National Criminal Justice Reference Service (NCJRS). NCJRS provides the largest criminal justice database in the world, publishing some of the foremost reports and information products available for crime and justice practitioners.[2]

www.ncstl.org. NIJ funds the National Clearinghouse for Science, Technology, and the Law (NCSTL), which offers an extensive database of scientific and legal publications. NCSTL helps NIJ develop training programs for lawyers and provides input to a number of NIJ's technical working groups and advisory committees.

Leading Through Conferences

NIJ hosts conferences that explore relevant and timely issues in criminal justice and technology research, often working collaboratively with other agencies. Key events in 2006 included:

The NIJ Conference. NIJ's annual conference brings together the Nation's top criminal justice practitioners, researchers, and policymakers to present research findings and advance justice administration. In 2006, more than 1,000 people attended the conference's 70 panels and workshops in Washington, DC.[3]

NIJ Operations Research Symposium. Operations research uses analytical methods, including modeling and simulation, to help managers make better decisions. NIJ challenged participants to solve relevant law enforcement problems; the winning solutions were presented at the meeting and served as the foundation for a lively discussion.

Science, Technology, and the Law Conference. A 2006 conference focused on the ever-evolving intersection of science, technology, and the law. Topics included driving-under-the-influence standards, identity theft, forensic psychology, methamphetamines, fingerprints, and biogeographic ancestry.

[1] See www.dna.gov/training.

[2] NCJRS has a toll-free number to answer questions that require an advanced knowledge of criminal justice topics: 1–800–851–3420.

[3] More information about the conference is available at www.ojp.usdoj.gov/nij/events/nij_conference/welcome.html.

Critical Incident Preparedness Conference. On September 6–8, 2006, the 8th Annual Technologies for Critical Incident Preparedness Conference and Exposition brought together more than 150 agencies and vendors to share technological advancements that aid responders in mass disasters and pandemic outbreaks. International and domestic experts explored a wide range of topics, such as preparing for epidemics, protecting the Nation's borders, responding to natural and terrorist disasters, creating technologies that advance police interoperability, and securing the Nation's transportation infrastructure.

Partners in Dissemination

NIJ's partnerships and collaborations with other public agencies, universities, and professional organizations help extend its outreach.

National Law Enforcement and Corrections Technology Center (NLECTC). *Specializing in electronic crime, rural law enforcement, distributing surplus property, and officer training, NLECTC's five regional centers deliver NIJ's research and technology to practitioners in the field. Police and corrections professionals use these facilities to get the tools and expertise they need to perform their jobs safely and efficiently. NLECTC's Web site, www.justnet.org, holds an extensive virtual library of criminal justice research.*

Forensic Resource Network. *The Forensic Resource Network is a collaborative hub of activity for crime laboratories, providing quality assurance for products, training forensic scientists, and disseminating information. Members include:*

- *National Forensic Science and Technology Center.*

- *Marshall University Forensic Science Center.*

- *National Center for Forensic Science.*

- *West Virginia University—Forensic Identification Program.*

Appendixes

'06

Appendix A

Financial Data

Exhibit A-1: NIJ's Research and Development Portfolio,
Awards Made FY 1996–2006

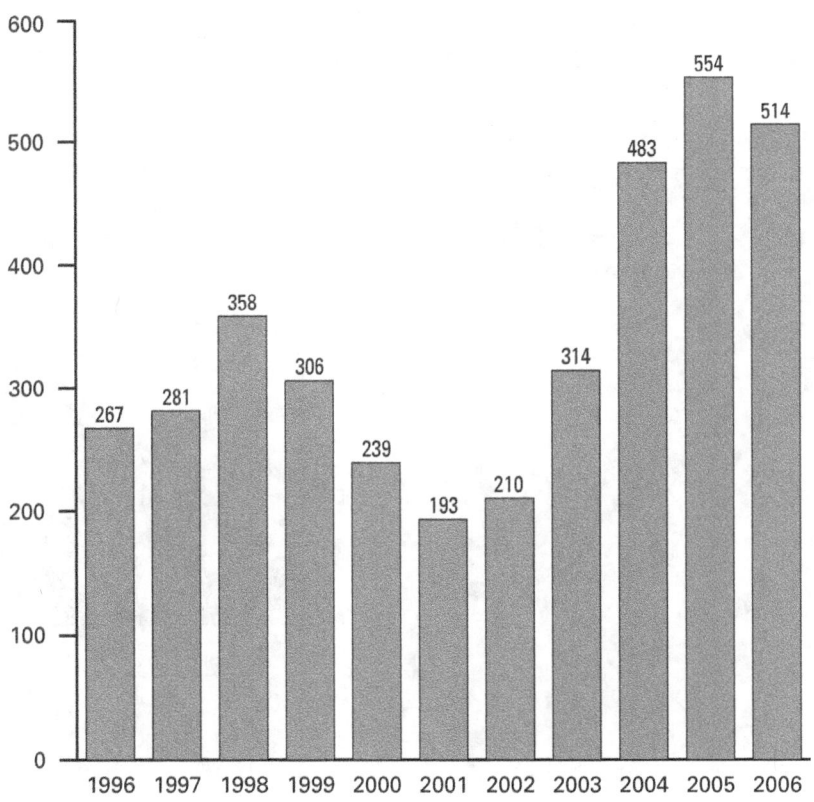

Exhibit A-2: Value of Active Awards, in Millions, FY 1996–2006

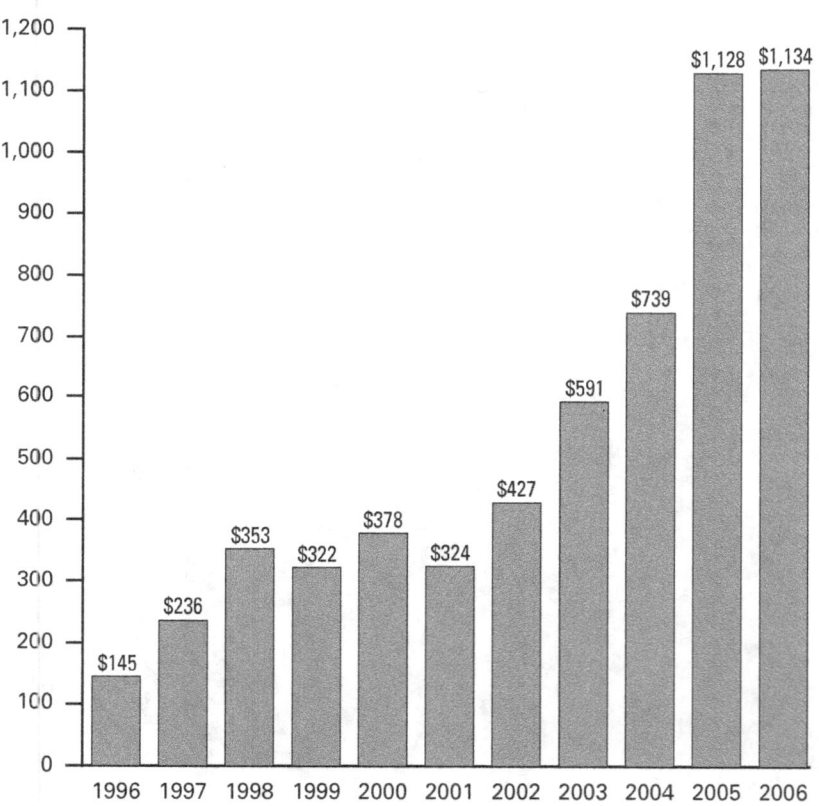

Exhibit A-3: Sources of NIJ Funds, in Millions, FY 1996–2006

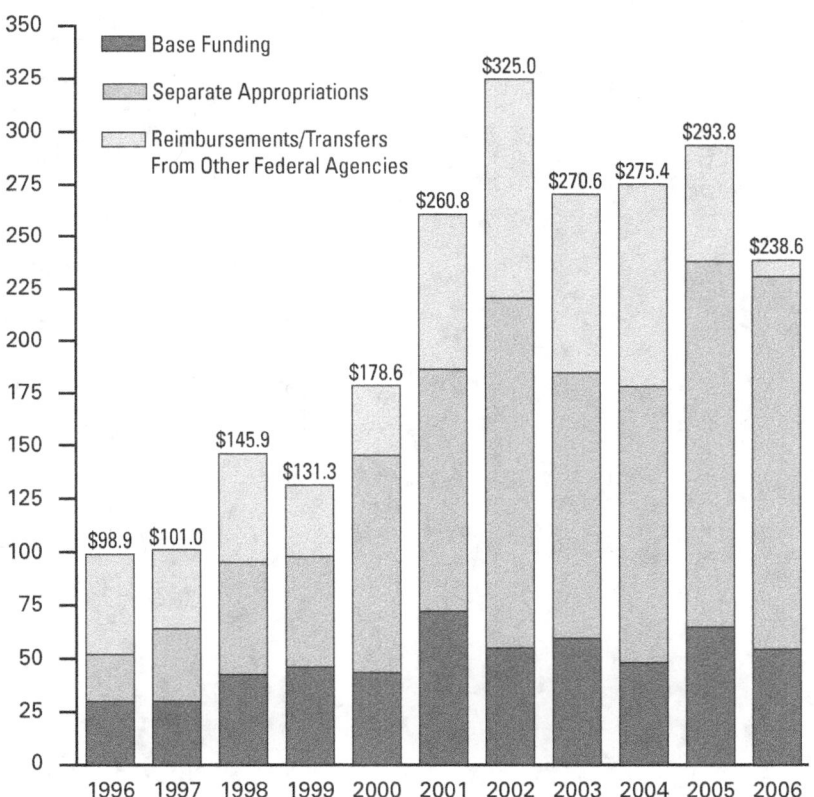

Exhibit A-4: Allocation of NIJ Funds as a Percentage of Total Funding,*
FY 2006

Social Science	Research	12%
	Evaluation	2%
Science and Technology	Capacity Enhancement**	39%
	Research and Development	20%
	Technology Assistance	12%
	Standards	3%
Program Support		4%
Dissemination		4%
Other		4%

*Total funding of $238.6 million includes NIJ base appropriation of $54.3 million plus separate appropriations and funds transfers.

**Grants to improve and enhance crime laboratories.

Exhibit A-5: DNA Funding, FY 2006

The funding request under the President's DNA Initiative was $107.1 million. Actual funding breakdowns for each purpose area are shown below.

DNA Capacity Enhancement	$42,466,626
DNA Casework Backlog Reduction	20,580,766
Convicted Offender DNA Backlog Reduction	16,010,111
Training for the Criminal Justice Community	4,003,430
Identifying Missing Persons	2,135,163
Research and Development	13,063,695
Earmarks*	8,885,052
Post-Rescission Total	$107,144,843

*Program carves out approximately $3,948,912 for the post-conviction testing grant program and approximately $4,936,140 for OLES for forensic science lab equipment standards and testing.

Appendix B

NIJ Awards in FY 2006 (includes first-time awards and supplements to previous awards)

Solicitation titles

- Biometrics Technologies
- Communications Technologies
- Congressional Directed Awards
- Convicted Offender DNA Backlog Reduction Program (In-House Analysis and Data Review)
- Corrections Technologies
- Crime and Justice Research
- Data Resources Program: Funding for Analysis of Existing Data
- Discretionary Awards
- Electronic Crime Research and Development
- Evaluation of OJJDP's Commercial Sexual Exploitation of Children Demonstration Program in Atlanta/Fulton County
- Evaluation of Public Safety Interventions
- Evaluation of Technology
- Forensic Casework DNA Backlog Reduction Program
- Forensic DNA Capacity Enhancement Program
- Forensic DNA Research and Development
- Forensic Toxicology Research and Development
- Forensics Science Research Targeting Forensic Engineering, Forensic Pathology, Forensic Odontology, Trace Evidence, Controlled Substances, and Questioned Documents
- Graduate Research Fellowship
- Information-Led Policing Research, Technology Development, and Testing and Evaluation
- Justice System Response to Intimate Partner Violence and Stalking
- Less-Lethal Technologies

- Modeling and Simulation Research and Development: Software for Improved Operations, Operational Modeling, Speech-to-Text Recognition, and Training Technologies
- Officer Safety Equipment
- Outcome Evaluations of Violence Prevention Programs
- Paul Coverdell Forensic Science Improvement Grant Program
- Process and Outcome Evaluation of G.R.E.A.T.
- Research and Development on Crime Scene Tools, Techniques, and Technologies
- Research and Development on Impression Evidence
- Research and Evaluation in Community Corrections: A Multijurisdictional Study of Reduced Caseload and Related Case Supervision Strategies in Managing Medium- and High-Risk Offenders
- Research and Evaluation on the Abuse, Neglect, and Exploitation of Elderly Individuals, Older Women, and Residents of Residential Care Facilities
- Research and Evaluation on Sexual Violence and Violent Behavior in Corrections
- School Safety Technologies
- Sensors and Surveillance Technologies
- Sexual Violence from Adolescence to Late Adulthood: Research, Evaluation, and the Criminal Justice Response
- Social Science Research on Terrorism
- Social Science Research on the Role and Impact of Forensic Evidence on the Criminal Justice Process
- Study of Administration of Justice in Indian Country
- Transnational Crime
- W.E.B. Dubois Fellowship

Awards by solicitation

Biometrics Technologies

Active 3-D Face Capture
General Electric Company
$499,699
2006–IJ–CX–K045

Face Recognition From Video
University of Notre Dame
$362,476
2006–IJ–CX–K041

Facial and Iris-Based Biometric System
New Jersey Institute of Technology
$191,281
2006–IJ–CX–K033

Use of HDTV for In-Vehicle Cameras: Surveillance and Biometrics
Purdue University
$201,852
2006–IJ–CX–K125

Communications Technologies

Agile, Multi-Antenna Capable SDR Platform for Advanced Public Safety Communications
University of California
$249,984
2006–IJ–CX–K044

Evaluating IEEE 802.16 Broadband Wireless as a Communications Infrastructure for Public Safety Activities
Clemson University
$150,000
2006–IJ–CX–K035

Software-Defined Emergency Radio
University of Texas–Dallas
$199,907
2006–IJ–CX–K043

Software-Defined Radio Technologies for Justice and Public Safety Communications
University of Notre Dame
$200,000
2006–IJ–CX–K034

Congressional Directed Awards

Advanced Law Enforcement Response Technology Systems
West Virginia High Technology Consortium Foundation
$4,442,526
2006–LT–BX–K002

Advanced Technologies for Law Enforcement
University of New Hampshire
$2,961,684
2006–IJ–CX–K022

Center for Criminal Justice Technology Systems Integration Projects
Mitretek Systems, Inc.
$1,954,985
2006–DD–BX–K015

Forensic Science Training and Technical Assistance
National Forensic Science Technology Center
$4,951,379
2006–MU–BX–K002

Maximizing the Capabilities of the Forensic Science Community
National Academy of Sciences
$1,480,842
2006–DN–BX–0001

Nontoxic Drug Detection and Identification Aerosol Technology
Mistral Security, Inc.
$740,421
2006–LT–BX–K001

Partnership for Uniting DNA and Fingerprint Identifications
University of Connecticut
$172,765
2006–DD–BX–K002

Convicted Offender DNA Backlog Reduction Program
(In-House Analysis and Data Review)

Alabama Department of Forensic Sciences
$396,000
2006–DN–BX–K234

Alaska Department of Public Safety
$87,500
2006–DN–BX–K235

California Department of Justice
$756,297
2006–DN–BX–K239

Georgia Bureau of Investigation
$294,000
2006–DN–BX–K248

Illinois State Police
$16,175
2006–DN–BX–K240

Kansas Bureau of Investigation
$248,238
2006–DN–BX–K237

Kentucky State Police
$73,381
2006–DN–BX–K236

Missouri State Highway Patrol
$254,471
2006–DN–BX–K241

New Jersey Department of Law and Public Safety
$615,829
2006–DN–BX–K242

New York State Police
$825,000
2006–DN–BX–K246

North Dakota Office of the Attorney General
$52,500
2006–DN–BX–K233

Oklahoma State Bureau of Investigation
$22,471
2006–DN–BX–K247

Pennsylvania State Police
$953,203
2006–DN–BX–K243

Texas Department of Public Safety
$1,517,288
2006–DN–BX–K244

Vermont Department of Public Safety
$76,843
2006–DN–BX–K245

Washington State Patrol
$480,412
2006–DN–BX–K238

Corrections Technologies

Cross-Functional Systemic Trend Mapping in Corrections
Florida Department of Corrections
$500,000
2006–IJ–CX–K007

Crime and Justice Research

Alcohol Availability, Distribution Policies, and Their Relationship to Crime and Alcohol-Related Injury
Urban Institute
$105,989
2006–IJ–CX–0012

Alternative Sentencing Policies for Drug Offenders: Evaluating the Effectiveness of Kansas Senate Bill 123
Vera Institute of Justice, Inc.
$273,897
2006–IJ–CX–0032

Crime and Justice Research
Arizona State University
$78,933
2006–IJ–CX–0016

Crime and Justice Research
Colorado, State of
$299,978
2006–IJ–CX–0015

Day Reporting Centers for Parolees in New Jersey: Evaluation of Efficacy
New Jersey State Parole Board
$218,965
2006–IJ–CX–0036

Do Best Practice Interviews With Child Abuse Victims Influence Case Outcomes?
Brooklyn College
$176,229
2006–IJ–CX–0019

Evaluation of the Processing of Habeas Corpus Cases in U.S. District Courts
Vanderbilt University
$257,747
2006–IJ–CX–0020

Long-Term Consequences of Delinquency: Child Maltreatment and Crime in Early Adulthood
New York Office of Children and Family Services
$290,386
2006–IJ–CX–0014

Megan's Law: An Empirical Analysis
New Jersey Department of Corrections
$38,252
2006–IJ–CX–0018

Multicity Assessment of Juvenile Delinquency in the United States: Expansion of the International Self-Report Delinquency Study
Northeastern University
$252,698
2006–IJ–CX–0045

Polyvictimization History Among Girls Adjudicated Delinquent
University of South Carolina
$297,888
2006–WG–BX–0011

Simultaneous Effects of Individual, Program, and Neighborhood Attributes on Juvenile Recidivism Using GIS and Spatial Data Mining
Temple University
$316,712
2006–IJ–CX–0022

Data Resources Program: Funding for Analysis of Existing Data

Effects of Incarceration on the Safety and Well-Being of Families and Inmates Using the Crime Victimization Survey
City University of New York
$34,997
2006–IJ–CX–0007

Effects of Prosecution on Violence Between Intimate Partners
Joint Centers for Justice Studies
$34,425
2006–IJ–CX–0005

Discretionary Awards

Application of Proteinases for DNA Isolation of Bone Specimens
Indiana University
$15,396
2006–DN–BX–K010

Border Counties Criminal Justice Cost Study
United States-Mexico Border Counties Foundation
$148,084
2006–DD–BX–0004

Border Research and Technology Center Support
Sheriffs Association of Texas
$1,375,497
2006–IJ–CX–K016

Breakable Cartridge Cyanocrylate Fingerprint Development System
Mountain State University
$82,820
2006–DN–BX–K037

Cell Phone Detector
South Carolina Research Authority
$200,000
2006–DE–BX–K007

Center for Quality Policing
Ranc Corporation
$493,614
2006–DD–BX–0025

Cyber Justice Gateway
Erin Kenneally
$300,000
2006–DE–BX–K001

E-Crime Investigative Technologies
Florida State University
$299,940
2006–DN–BX–K007

Electronic Control Weapons and Unexpected Deaths-in-Custody
International Association of Chiefs of Police
$257,638
2006–IJ–CX–K046

Event Dynamics and the Role of Third Parties in Youth Violence
Ohio State University
$259,756
2006–IJ–CX–0004

GLOBAL Personnel
Space and Naval Warfare Systems Center
$325,000
2006–IA–A6–6220

Governors' Criminal Justice Policy Advisors Project
National Governors Association
$250,000
2006–IJ–CX–0039

IACP Research Advisory Committee
International Association of Chiefs of Police
$125,000
2006–IJ–CX–0031

In-Car Video Technical Support
Institute for Forensic Imaging Foundation, Inc.
$74,640
2006–IJ–CX–K003

Internet Forensics Toolkit for Law Enforcement
University of California–San Diego
$40,000
2006–IJ–CX–K036

Interoperability of AFIS Systems for Latent Print Searches
International Association for Identification
$179,943
2006–DN–BX–K249

Jihad, Crime, and the Internet
University of Illinois
$275,802
2006–IJ–CX–0038

Louisiana Hurricane DNA Identification Effort
Louisiana State Police
$1,000,000
2006–IJ–CX–K001

Mobile Phone Forensics Software and Hardware Development and Training
Margaret Jeitner
$205,000
2006–DN–BX–K020

Offender Supervision With Electronic Technology
Bureau of Justice Assistance
$50,000
2006–IA–A6–6227

Probability of a Match in Bite Marks
Institute for Forensic Imaging
$96,903
2006–DN–BX–K252

Recognition of Noncooperative Individuals Using 3-D Face Biometrics
University of Southern California
$498,000
2006–DE–BX–K006

South Carolina Information Exchange: Orangeburg County Project
South Carolina Research Authority
$148,084
2006–LT–BX–K004

Technology Transfer of Forensic Document Analysis System
CedarTech, Inc.
$153,289
2006–DN–BX–K025

Electronic Crime Research and Development

Automated Human Image Detection and Authentication
University of Rhode Island
$199,957
2006–DN–BX–K023

Automated Steganography Detection and Breaking for Law Enforcement
University of Rhode Island
$399,836
2006–DN–BX–K022

File Hound: A Law Enforcement Investigative Tool
Purdue University
$197,589
2006–DN–BX–K250

File Marshall: Automatic Analysis of Peer-to-Peer Usage
Odyssey Research Associates, Inc.
$370,121
2006–DN–BX–K013

FREEAK: Forensic Rapid Evidence Extraction and Analysis Kit for Immediate Personal Digital Technology Forensics
Purdue University
$237,540
2006–IJ–CX–K020

Evaluation of OJJDP's Commercial Sexual Exploitation of Children Demonstration Program in Atlanta/Fulton County

Evaluation of OJJDP's Commercial Sexual Exploitation of Children Demonstration Project
Georgia State University
$451,864
2006–JE–FX–0006

Evaluation of Public Safety Interventions

Eliminating Street Drug Markets: A Process and Outcome Evaluation
University of North Carolina–Greensboro
$283,001
2006–IJ–CX–0034

Evaluation of Gang Hot-Spots Policing in Chicago
Chicago Police Department
$250,000
2006–IJ–CX–0023

Evaluation of One Vision, One Life
Rand Corporation
$249,116
2006–IJ–CX–0030

Evaluation of Target's Safe City Initiative: An Action-Research Crime Prevention Partnership
Urban Institute
$246,597
2006–IJ–CX–0021

Evaluation of Technology

Evaluation of Less-Lethal Technologies on Police Use-of-Force Outcomes
Police Executive Research Forum
$406,734
2006–IJ–CX–0028

Forensic Casework DNA Backlog Reduction Program

Alabama Department of Forensic Sciences
$357,181
2006–DN–BX–K038

Alameda County
$103,485
2006–DN–BX–K093

Alaska Department of Public Safety
$106,474
2006–DN–BX–K033

Albuquerque Police Department
$107,923
2006–DN–BX–K061

Allegheny County
$67,444
2006–DN–BX–K039

Arizona Criminal Justice Commission
$244,503
2006–DN–BX–K040

Arizona Department of Public Safety
$168,868
2006–DN–BX–K041

Arkansas State Crime Laboratory
$73,128
2006–DN–BX–K042

Austin, City of
$60,730
2006–DN–BX–K062

Baltimore Police Department
$97,713
2006–DN–BX–K063

Boston, City of
$84,522
2006–DN–BX–K064

Broward County Sheriff's Office
$101,862
2006–DN–BX–K058

Connecticut Department of Public Safety
$145,843
2006–DN–BX–K086

Contra Costa County
$94,890
2006–DN–BX–K092

Cuyahoga County Coroner's Office
$75,000
2006–DN–BX–K091

Dallas County
$210,910
2006–DN–BX–K084

Denver, City and County of
$58,725
2006–DN–BX–K059

District of Columbia Metropolitan
Police Department
$75,158
2006–DN–BX–K099

Erie County
$77,978
2006–DN–BX–K094

Florida Department of Law Enforcement
$947,192
2006–DN–BX–K087

Fresno County Sheriff's Department
$90,000
2006–DN–BX–K109

Georgia Bureau of Investigation
$536,845
2006–DN–BX–K110

Harris County
$508,498
2006–DN–BX–K111

Hennepin County Sheriff's Office
$41,810
2006–DN–BX–K112

Illinois State Police
$850,000
2006–DN–BX–K083

Indiana State Police
$307,146
2006–DN–BX–K107

Indianapolis-Marion County Forensic Services
Agency
$72,046
2006–DN–BX–K108

Instituto de Ciencias Forenses de Puerto Rico
$177,517
2006–DN–BX–K105

Johnson County Criminalistics Laboratory
$67,656
2006–DN–BX–K106

Kansas Bureau of Investigation
$151,580
2006–DN–BX–K104

Kansas City Board of Police Commissioners
$135,697
2006–DN–BX–K057

Kentucky State Police
$263,695
2006–DN–BX–K097

Kern County
$90,407
2006–DN–BX–K095

Los Angeles, City of
$498,570
2006–DN–BX–K065

Los Angeles County Sheriff's Department
$180,000
2006–DN–BX–K102

Louisiana State Police
$391,897
2006–DN–BX–K103

Mansfield, City of
$70,000
2006–DN–BX–K066

Maryland State Police
$72,975
2006–DN–BX–K101

Massachusetts State Police
$267,342
2006–DN–BX–K100

Miami-Dade County Police Department
$200,323
2006–DN–BX–K052

Michigan State Police
$1,096,775
2006–DN–BX–K044

Minnesota Bureau of Criminal Apprehension
$293,234
2006–DN–BX–K043

Mississippi Department of Public Safety
$248,381
2006–DN–BX–K098

Missouri State Highway Patrol
$82,516
2006–DN–BX–K051

Monroe County
$60,194
2006–DN–BX–K050

Montana Department of Justice
$54,221
2006–DN–BX–K085

Montgomery County
$50,000
2006–DN–BX–K049

Montgomery County Police Department
$45,775
2006–DN–BX–K048

Nassau County
$24,222
2006–DN–BX–K082

Nebraska State Patrol
$118,106
2006–DN–BX–K081

New Hampshire Department of Safety
$18,220
2006–DN–BX–K080

New Jersey Department of Law
and Public Safety
$308,328
2006–DN–BX–K079

New Mexico, State of
$45,000
2006–DN–BX–K113

New York, City of
$331,946
2006–DN–BX–K067

New York State Police
$203,919
2006–DN–BX–K078

North Carolina Department of Crime Control
and Public Safety
$513,761
2006–DN–BX–K076

North Dakota Office of the Attorney General
$30,063
2006–DN–BX–K077

Northern Illinois Police
$43,311
2006–DN–BX–K075

Oakland, City of
$84,874
2006–DN–BX–K122

Ohio Office of the Attorney General
$728,911
2006–DN–BX–K119

Oklahoma State Bureau of Investigation
$38,219
2006–DN–BX–K074

Onondaga County Health Department
$24,093
2006–DN–BX–K072

Palm Beach County Sheriff's Office
$103,115
2006–DN–BX–K071

Philadelphia, City of
$681,455
2006–DN–BX–K115

Prince George's County Police Department
$92,782
2006–DN–BX–K070

Richland County
$26,205
2006–DN–BX–K117

Sacramento County District Attorney
$200,858
2006–DN–BX–K068

San Bernardino County Sheriff-Coroner
$208,007
2006–DN–BX–K096

San Diego County
$148,193
2006–DN–BX–K069

San Diego Police Department
$140,374
2006–DN–BX–K121

San Francisco, City and County of
$104,231
2006–DN–BX–K060

San Mateo County
$41,757
2006–DN–BX–K047

Santa Clara County
$98,123
2006–DN–BX–K088

South Carolina Law Enforcement Division
$332,766
2006–DN–BX–K114

South Dakota Division of Criminal
Investigation
$63,706
2006–DN–BX–K073

St. Louis County Police Department
$42,455
2006–DN–BX–K045

St. Louis Metropolitan Police Department
$67,345
2006–DN–BX–K046

Suffolk County
$28,568
2006–DN–BX–K118

Texas, State of
$788,300
2006–DN–BX–K116

University of North Texas Health Science
Center–Fort Worth
$155,314
2006–DN–BX–K056

Ventura County Sheriff's Office
$41,139
2006–DN–BX–K089

Vermont Department of Public Safety
$30,063
2006–DN–BX–K123

Virginia Department of Forensic Science
$385,992
2006–DN–BX–K120

Washington State Patrol
$545,256
2006–DN–BX–K053

West Virginia State Police
$69,432
2006–DN–BX–K054

Westchester County
$24,053
2006–DN–BX–K090

Wisconsin Department of Justice
$230,844
2006–DN–BX–K055

Forensic DNA Capacity Enhancement Program

Alabama Department of Forensic Sciences
$711,269
2006–DN–BX–K215

Alameda County
$136,825
2006–DN–BX–K152

Alaska Department of Public Safety
$212,026
2006–DN–BX–K216

Allegheny County
$102,588
2006–DN–BX–K217

Anne Arundel County Police Department
$48,988
2006–DN–BX–K151

Arizona Criminal Justice Commission
$481,397
2006–DN–BX–K149

Arizona Department of Public Safety
$341,764
2006–DN–BX–K150

Arkansas State Crime Laboratory
$478,218
2006–DN–BX–K148

Austin, City of
$145,710
2006–DN–BX–K143

Baltimore City Police Department
$194,394
2006–DN–BX–K166

Boston Police Department
$135,771
2006–DN–BX–K165

Broward County Sheriff's Office
$202,766
2006–DN–BX–K145

California Department of Justice
$972,915
2006–DN–BX–K146

Charlotte-Mecklenburg Police Department
$107,210
2006–DN–BX–K164

Colorado Department of Public Safety
$652,289
2006–DN–BX–K157

Columbus Police Department
$72,013
2006–DN–BX–K163

Connecticut Department of Public Safety
$290,423
2006–DN–BX–K170

Contra Costa County
$136,825
2006–DN–BX–K154

Cuyahoga County Coroner's Office
$216,039
2006–DN–BX–K173

Dallas County
$502,447
2006–DN–BX–K171

Delaware Health and Social Services
$128,998
2006–DN–BX–K172

Denver Police Department
$117,064
2006–DN–BX–K144

District of Columbia Metropolitan Police Department
$149,666
2006–DN–BX–K208

DuPage County Office of the Sheriff
$53,371
2006–DN–BX–K168

Erie County
$155,424
2006–DN–BX–K180

Florida Department of Law Enforcement
$1,886,239
2006–DN–BX–K167

Georgia Bureau of Investigation
$1,069,041
2006–DN–BX–K196

Hamilton County
$72,013
2006–DN–BX–K195

Harris County
$437,306
2006–DN–BX–K194

Hennepin County Sheriff's Office
$150,745
2006–DN–BX–K192

Idaho State Police
$213,808
2006–DN–BX–K193

Illinois State Police
$1,668,051
2006–DN–BX–K191

Indiana State Police
$604,079
2006–DN–BX–K189

Indianapolis-Marion County Forensic
Services Agency
$151,020
2006–DN–BX–K190

Johnson County
$102,553
2006–DN–BX–K188

Kansas Bureau of Investigation
$276,300
2006–DN–BX–K186

Kansas City Board of Police Commissioners
$261,576
2006–DN–BX–K147

Kentucky State Police
$525,255
2006–DN–BX–K155

Kern County
$136,825
2006–DN–BX–K181

Lake County
$36,007
2006–DN–BX–K187

Las Vegas Metropolitan Police Department
$181,261
2006–DN–BX–K185

Los Angeles, City of
$564,048
2006–DN–BX–K162

Los Angeles County Sheriff's Department
$658,315
2006–DN–BX–K184

Louisiana State Police
$780,400
2006–DN–BX–K183

Maine Department of Public Safety
$118,664
2006–DN–BX–K210

Mansfield, City of
$72,013
2006–DN–BX–K160

Maryland State Police
$159,335
2006–DN–BX–K211

Massachusetts State Police
$565,520
2006–DN–BX–K209

Miami-Dade County Police Department
$398,922
2006–DN–BX–K207

Michigan State Police
$2,184,050
2006–DN–BX–K132

Minnesota Bureau of Criminal Apprehension
$646,047
2006–DN–BX–K229

Mississippi Department of Public Safety
$494,610
2006–DN–BX–K206

Missouri Southern State University
$30,814
2006–DN–BX–K182

Missouri State Highway Patrol
$169,483
2006–DN–BX–K204

Monroe County
$119,977
2006–DN–BX–K205

Montana Department of Justice
$107,973
2006–DN–BX–K169

Montgomery County
$624,657
2006–DN–BX–K141

Montgomery County Police Department
$82,206
2006–DN–BX–K203

Nassau County
$48,278
2006–DN–BX–K139

Nebraska State Patrol
$235,189
2006–DN–BX–K140

New Hampshire Department of Safety
$169,977
2006–DN–BX–K138

New Jersey Department of Law
and Public Safety
$613,986
2006–DN–BX–K137

New Mexico, State of
$430,467
2006–DN–BX–K133

New York, City of
$720,788
2006–DN–BX–K161

New York State Police
$406,442
2006–DN–BX–K135

North Carolina Department of Crime Control
and Public Safety
$915,862
2006–DN–BX–K136

North Dakota Office of the Attorney General
$59,866
2006–DN–BX–K218

Northern Illinois Police
$57,463
2006–DN–BX–K219

Oakland, City of
$136,825
2006–DN–BX–K159

Ohio Office of the Attorney General
$747,078
2006-DN-BX-K230

Oklahoma State Bureau of Investigation
$621,113
2006-DN-BX-K221

Onondaga County Health Department
$46,707
2006-DN-BX-K222

Orange County
$199,767
2006-DN-BX-K179

Oregon State Police
$489,264
2006-DN-BX-K223

Palm Beach County Sheriff's Office
$205,343
2006-DN-BX-K224

Pennsylvania State Police
$871,914
2006-DN-BX-K202

Philadelphia Police Department
$516,810
2006-DN-BX-K158

Prince George's County Police Department
$169,687
2006-DN-BX-K201

Rhode Island Department of Health
$123,296
2006-DN-BX-K200

Richland County
$48,632
2006-DN-BX-K199

Sacramento County District Attorney
$227,236
2006-DN-BX-K198

San Bernardino County Sheriff-Coroner
$235,321
2006-DN-BX-K177

San Diego County
$167,652
2006-DN-BX-K197

San Diego Police Department
$158,805
2006-DN-BX-K156

San Francisco, City and County of
$136,825
2006-DN-BX-K142

San Mateo County
$136,825
2006-DN-BX-K225

Santa Clara County
$136,825
2006-DN-BX-K178

Sedgwick County
$58,385
2006-DN-BX-K176

South Carolina Law Enforcement Division
$666,200
2006-DN-BX-K226

South Dakota Office of the Attorney General
$126,860
2006-DN-BX-K220

St. Charles County Sheriff's Department
$21,477
2006-DN-BX-K227

St. Louis County Police Department
$64,783
2006-DN-BX-K134

St. Louis Metropolitan Police Department
$105,051
2006-DN-BX-K228

Suffolk County
$56,918
2006-DN-BX-K231

Tarrant County
$316,681
2006-DN-BX-K127

Texas, State of
$1,253,871
2006-DN-BX-K131

University of North Texas Health Science
Center-Fort Worth
$819,081
2006-DN-BX-K129

Utah Department of Public Safety
$348,864
2006-DN-BX-K212

Ventura Sheriff's Office
$136,825
2006-DN-BX-K174

Vermont Department of Public Safety
$59,866
2006-DN-BX-K232

Virginia Department of Forensic Science
$768,640
2006-DN-BX-K153

Washington State Patrol
$1,085,789
2006-DN-BX-K213

Washoe County Sheriff's Office
$219,986
2006-DN-BX-K128

West Virginia State Police
$138,263
2006-DN-BX-K130

Westchester County
$47,958
2006-DN-BX-K175

Wisconsin Department of Justice
$459,688
2006-DN-BX-K214

Forensic DNA Research and Development

Analysis of DNA Forensic Markers Using High Throughput Mass Spectrometry
Isis Pharmaceuticals, Inc.
$451,382
2006–DN–BX–K011

Double-Strand Break Repair of Highly Degraded DNA
University of Central Florida
$174,025
2006–DN–BX–K005

Effect of DNA Degradation and Inhibition on PCR Amplification of Single-Source and Mixed Forensic Samples
Florida International University
$347,399
2006–DN–BX–K006

Isolation of Highly Specific Protein Markers for the Identification of Biological Stains: Adapting Comparative Proteomics to Forensics
University of Denver
$186,602
2006–DN–BX–K001

Laser Microdissection as a Technique to Isolate Sperm Cells and Improve the Analysis of Touch Evidence
Bode Technology Group, Inc.
$191,429
2006–DN–BX–K032

Repair of DNA for Forensic Analysis
General Electric Company
$453,472
2006–DN–BX–K018

Separation of Sperm and Epithelial Cells in a Microfluidic Device: An Automated Method for High-Efficiency, High-Purity Separations
University of Virginia
$324,104
2006–DN–BX–K021

Forensic Toxicology Research and Development

Analysis of Cocaine Analytes in Human Hair: Evaluation of Concentration Ratios in Different Hair Types, Cocaine Sources, Drug User Populations, and Surface-Contaminated Specimens
Research Triangle Institute
$200,307
2006–DN–BX–K019

Development of Reference Materials for Control and Calibration of Hair Drug Testing
Research Triangle Institute
$212,344
2006–DN–BX–K012

LC/MS/MS Capabilities to Analyze Toxicology Postmortem Samples
Georgia Bureau of Investigation
$136,220
2006–DN–BX–K015

New and Novel Direct Sample Introduction, Time of Flight Mass Spectrometry Instrument for Postmortem Toxicology Screening
Research Triangle Institute
$484,545
2006–DN–BX–K014

Forensics Science Research Targeting Forensic Engineering, Forensic Pathology, Forensic Odontology, Trace Evidence, Controlled Substances, and Questioned Documents

Advanced Raman Spectroscopy Methods and Databases for the Evaluation of Trace Evidence and Examination of Questioned Documents
City University of New York
$311,948
2006–DN–BX–K034

Application of Fluorescence Line Narrowing Spectrosocopy to Forensic Fiber Examination
University of Central Florida
$185,476
2006–DN–BX–K036

Application of Laser-Induced Breakdown Spectroscopy to Forensic Science: Analysis of Paint Samples
University of Central Florida
$167,227
2006–DN–BX–K251

Forensic Analysis of Ink, Arson, Explosive, and Controlled-Substance Samples Using a Revolutionary Mass Spectrometry Method
Iowa State University
$414,145
2006–DN–BX–K017

Synthesis and Analytical Profiles for Regiosomeric and Isobaric Amines Related to MDMA, MDEA, and MBDB: Differentiation of Drug and Non-Drug Substances of Mass Spectral Equivalence
Auburn University
$533,746
2006–DN–BX–K016

Test of the Lamendin Age Estimation Method
State University of New York–Oswego
$6,915
2006–DN–BX–K035

Triacetone Triperoxide Synthetic Byproducts for Source and Route Determination
University of Central Florida
$257,134
2006–DN–BX–K009

Graduate Research Fellowship

Estimable Dynamic Model of Criminal Behavior
University of California–Los Angeles
$20,000
2006–IJ–CX–0002

Intersection of Genes, the Environment, and Crime and Delinquency: A Longitudinal Study of Offending
University of Cincinnati
$20,000
2006–IJ–CX–0001

Local Actors and U.S. Anti-Trafficking Policy: Interpretation, Mediation, and Implementation
Columbia University
$20,000
2006–IJ–CX–0003

Mitochondrial DNA Mixture Separation Development and Validation by Denaturing High-Performance Liquid Chromatography
University of Denver
$20,000
2006–DN–BX–K002

Information-Led Policing Research, Technology Development, and Testing and Evaluation

Detecting the Near-Repeat Phenomenon in Local and Regional Crime Data
Temple University
$95,350
2006–IJ–CX–K006

Evaluation of the County Justice Information Exchange Project
County Commissioners Association of Pennsylvania
$122,287
2006–IJ–CX–K027

SmartSearch: Automating Law Enforcement Searches Using GJXDM-Compliant Transactions
Automated Regional Justice Information Systems
$399,135
2006–IJ–CX–K042

Justice System Response to Intimate Partner Violence and Stalking

Crime Control Effects of Prosecuting Intimate Partner Violence
Joint Centers for Justice Studies
$113,203
2006–WG–BX–0004

Domestic Violence Courts: A National Portrait
New York, City of
$275,064
2006–WG–BX–0001

Intimate Partner Violence: Justice System Response and Public Health Service Utilization in a National Sample
University of Colorado
$279,955
2006–WG–BX–0003

Justice System Response to Intimate Partner Violence
University of Minnesota
$370,966
2006–WG–BX–0006

Model of Domestic Abuse Against Older Women and Barriers to Seeking Help
Florida International University
$469,590
2006–WG–BX–0008

Victim Participation in Intimate Partner Violence Prosecution: Implications for Safety
University of Pennsylvania
$498,726
2006–WG–BX–0007

Less-Lethal Technologies

Injuries Produced by Law Enforcement's Use of Less-Lethal Weapons
Wake Forest University Health Sciences
$149,804
2006–DE–BX–K002

Modeling and Simulation Research and Development: Software for Improved Operations, Operational Modeling, Speech-to-Text Recognition, and Training Technologies

A Bayesian Data Trawler for Urban Public Safety
Structured Decisions Corporation
$350,000
2006–IJ–CX–K011

Using Portable Radios to Operate Mobile Data Terminals
Portland State University
$158,356
2006–IJ–CX–K012

Officer Safety Equipment

Evaluation of Chemical and Electrical Flare Systems
Florida Gulf Coast University
$32,015
2006–IJ–CX–K008

Officer Safety Equipment
Blackhawk Industries Products Group
$174,600
2006–IJ–CX–K039

Use of a Strobe Personnel Tracking System in Officer Foot Pursuits and Perimeter Searches
Florida Gulf Coast University
$43,849
2006–IJ–CX–K009

Outcome Evaluations of Violence Prevention Programs

Evaluation of SAFEChildren, a Family-Focused Prevention Program
University of Illinois
$836,328
2006–JP–FX–0062

Outcome Evaluation of Tribes Learning Communities
WestEd
$658,303
2006–JP–FX–0059

Randomized Trial of Healthy Families New York: Does It Prevent Child Maltreatment?
New York Office of Children and Family Services
$648,056
2006–MU–MU–0002

Paul Coverdell Forensic Science Improvement Grant Program

Alabama Department of Economic
and Community Affairs
$155,450
2006–DN–BX–0014

Alaska Department of Public Safety
$91,015
2006–DN–BX–0012

Anchorage, Municipality of
$95,000
2006–DN–BX–0013

Anne Arundel County
$65,598
2006–DN–BX–0015

Arizona Criminal Justice Commission
$202,568
2006–DN–BX–0016

Arkansas Department of Finance
and Administration
$94,787
2006–DN–BX–0017

Austin Police Department
$94,100
2006–DN–BX–0022

Baltimore, City of
$93,200
2006–DN–BX–0023

Broome County
$94,803
2006–DN–BX–0018

California Governor's Office of Emergency
Services
$1,232,336
2006–DN–BX–0020

Cherokee County
$73,151
2006–DN–BX–0021

Cleveland Police
$95,000
2006–DN–BX–0024

Colorado Division of Criminal Justice
$159,112
2006–DN–BX–0040

Colorado Springs, City of
$51,650
2006–DN–BX–0025

Connecticut, State of
$119,723
2006–DN–BX–0077

Dallas County
$95,000
2006–DN–BX–0037

Delaware Criminal Justice Council
$91,015
2006–DN–BX–0038

District of Columbia Justice Grants
Administration
$91,015
2006–DN–BX–0039

Fairfax County
$94,435
2006–DN–BX–0034

Florida Department of Law Enforcement
$606,747
2006–DN–BX–0041

Fort Worth, City of
$95,000
2006–DN–BX–0026

Gainesville Police Department
$62,146
2006–DN–BX–0027

Georgia Criminal Justice Coordinating Council
$386,482
2006–DN–BX–0042

Guam, Territory of
$91,015
2006–DN–BX–0044

Hawaii Department of the Attorney General
$91,015
2006–DN–BX–0045

Hillsboro, City of
$84,450
2006–DN–BX–0019

Hillsborough County
$95,000
2006–DN–BX–0046

Houston Police Department
$95,000
2006–DN–BX–0028

Idaho State Police
$91,015
2006–DN–BX–0047

Illinois Criminal Justice Information Authority
$435,312
2006–DN–BX–0048

Indiana Criminal Justice Institute
$213,914
2006–DN–BX–0049

Instituto de Ciencias Forenses de Puerto Rico
$133,400
2006–DN–BX–0050

Iowa Governor's Office of Drug Control Policy
$101,171
2006–DN–BX–0051

Jefferson County
$82,349
2006–DN–BX–0052

Johnson County
$90,000
2006–DN–BX–0053

Kansas Office of the Governor
$93,611
2006–DN–BX–0069

Kenosha County Department of
Human Services
$93,410
2006–DN–BX–0054

Kentucky Justice and Safety Cabinet
$142,340
2006–DN–BX–0055

Lane County
$94,988
2006–DN–BX–0056

Louisiana Commission on Law Enforcement
and Administration of Justice
$154,284
2006–DN–BX–0057

Maine, State of
$82,639
2006–DN–BX–0005

Maine, State of
$91,015
2006–DN–BX–0078

Maricopa County
$95,000
2006–DN–BX–0058

Maryland Governor's Office of Crime
Control and Prevention
$191,009
2006–DN–BX–0043

Massachusetts State Police
$305,476
2006–DN–BX–0059

Miami Police Department
$95,000
2006–DN–BX–0029

Michigan, State of
$345,186
2006–DN–BX–0079

Minneapolis, City of
$95,000
2006–DN–BX–0030

Minnesota Department of Public Safety
$175,061
2006–DN–BX–0007

Mississippi Department of Public Safety
$99,628
2006–DN–BX–0009

Missouri Department of Public Safety
$197,827
2006–DN–BX–0060

Monroe County Medical Examiner
$51,034
2006–DN–BX–0061

Montana Board of Crime Control
$91,015
2006–DN–BX–0062

Nassau County
$95,000
2006–DN–BX–0063

Nebraska State Patrol
$91,015
2006–DN–BX–0011

New Hampshire, State of
$91,015
2006–DN–BX–0080

New Jersey Department of Law and
Public Safety
$297,337
2006–DN–BX–0064

New Mexico Department of Public Safety
$167,818
2006–DN–BX–0010

New York State Division of Criminal Justice
Services
$751,705
2006–DN–BX–0065

North Carolina Department of Crime Control
and Public Safety
$296,154
2006–DN–BX–0066

North Dakota Crime Laboratory Division
$104,085
2006–DN–BX–0067

North Miami, City of
$80,000
2006–DN–BX–0031

Ohio Office of Criminal Justice Services
$485,997
2006–DN–BX–0070

Oklahoma District Attorneys Council
$216,005
2006–DN–BX–0071

Oregon State Police
$219,183
2006–DN–BX–0008

Pennsylvania Commission on Crime
and Delinquency
$423,929
2006–DN–BX–0072

Rapid City Police Department
$93,855
2006–DN–BX–0032

Rhode Island, State of
$91,015
2006–DN–BX–0081

Sedgwick County
$95,000
2006–DN–BX–0073

South Carolina Department of Public Safety
$145,125
2006–DN–BX–0074

South Dakota Office of the Attorney General
$124,353
2006–DN–BX–0068

Spokane County Medical Examiner
$94,233
2006–DN–BX–0075

St. Louis Metropolitan Police Department
$84,385
2006–DN–BX–0076

Tennessee, State of
$203,375
2006–DN–BX–0082

Texas, State of
$779,670
2006–DN–BX–0083

Tooele City Corporation
$82,007
2006–DN–BX–0084

Twin Falls County
$95,000
2006–DN–BX–0085

Utah Department of Public Safety
$93,424
2006–DN–BX–0086

Utica, City of
$43,975
2006–DN–BX–0033

Ventura County
$95,000
2006–DN–BX–0035

Vermont Department of Public Safety
$91,015
2006–DN–BX–0087

Virgin Islands, Territory of
$91,015
2006–DN–BX–0088

Virginia Department of Criminal
Justice Services
$258,099
2006–DN–BX–0089

Washington Department of Community,
Trade, and Economic Development
$214,453
2006–DN–BX–0090

West Virginia Division of Criminal
Justice Services
$120,561
2006–DN–BX–0091

Westchester County
$72,560
2006–DN–BX–0036

Wisconsin Department of Justice
$188,820
2006–DN–BX–0092

Wyoming Office of the Attorney General
$91,015
2006–DN–BX–0093

Process and Outcome Evaluation of G.R.E.A.T.

Process and Outcome Evaluation of G.R.E.A.T.
University of Missouri–St. Louis
$2,497,585
2006–JV–FX–0011

Research and Development on Crime Scene Tools, Techniques, and Technologies

Development of an Optical Handheld Biological Evidence Detection System
MicroBioSystems of Utah
$324,547
2006–DN–BX–K028

Enhanced Visualization of Bloodstains
John Jay College
$123,311
2006–DN–BX–K026

Field Detection of Drug and Explosive Odor Signatures Using SPME–IMS
Florida International University
$249,446
2006–DN–BX–K027

Research and Development on Impression Evidence

Enhancing the Quality of Aged Fingerprints Developed by Cyanoacrylate Fuming
University of Tennessee
$126,505
2006–DN–BX–K031

Statistical Validation of the Individuality of Guns Using High-Resolution Topographical Images of Bullets
Intelligent Automation, Inc.
$102,798
2006–DN–BX–K030

Statistical Validation of the Individuality of Tool Marks Due to the Effect of Wear, Environmental Exposure, and Partial Evidence
Intelligent Automation, Inc.
$149,477
2006–DN–BX–K029

Research and Evaluation in Community Corrections: A Multijurisdictional Study of Reduced Caseload and Related Case Supervision Strategies in Managing Medium- and High-Risk Offenders

Multijurisdictional Study of Reduced Caseload and Related Supervision Strategies in Managing Offenders on Probation
Abt Associates Inc.
$999,940
2006–IJ–CX–0011

Research and Evaluation on the Abuse, Neglect, and Exploitation of Elderly Individuals, Older Women, and Residents of Residential Care Facilities

Financial Abuse of the Elderly Versus Other Forms of Elder Abuse: Assessing the Dynamics, Risk Factors, and Society's Response
University of Virginia
$290,414
2006–WG–BX–0010

Measuring the Financial Exploitation and Psychological Abuse of Elderly Individuals
University of Illinois
$304,300
2006–MU–MU–0004

Multisite Study to Characterize Pressure Ulcers in Long-Term Care Under Best Practices
University of California
$561,718
2006–IJ–CX–0029

Statewide Analysis of Elder Abuse
Advocates for Human Potential
$118,376
2006–WG–BX–0009

Research on Sexual Violence and Violent Behavior in Corrections

Application of Situational Crime Prevention to Sexual Assaults in Jail Facilities: An Action-Research Partnership
Urban Institute
$496,704
2006–RP–BX–0040

Gender Violence and Safety: Improving Security in Women's Facilities
California State University–Fresno
$558,916
2006–RP–BX–0016

School Safety Technologies

School Safety and Sex Offender Screening Project
Raptor Technologies, Inc.
$52,675
2006–IJ–CX–0043

SharpRIDE
AEPCO, Inc.
$189,949
2006–IJ–CX–0042

Sensors and Surveillance Technologies

Handheld and Portable Sub-mmW Concealed Weapon Detection Sensors
Raytheon Company
$341,261
2006–IJ–CX–K024

Through-Wall Personnel Detector
Armadar, LLC
$275,000
2006–IJ–CX–K025

Through-Wall Surveillance for Locating Individuals Within Buildings
Time Domain Corporation
$199,966
2006–IJ–CX–K026

Weapons and Nonpermitted Device Detector
Luna Innovations, Inc.
$464,907
2006–IJ–CX–K023

Sexual Violence from Adolescence to Late Adulthood: Research, Evaluation, and the Criminal Justice Response

Effectiveness of Sex Offender Registration and Notification Policies in Reducing Sexual Violence Against Women
Medical University of South Carolina
$484,106
2006–WG–BX–0002

Sexual Assault Among Latinas Project
University of New Hampshire
$450,585
2006–WG–BX–0005

Social Science Research on Terrorism

Operation and Structure of Right-Wing Extremist Groups
University of Nebraska–Omaha
$144,140
2006–IJ–CX–0027

Organizational Learning and Islamic Extremism
Pennsylvania State University
$148,862
2006–IJ–CX–0025

Prosecution of Terrorism Cases
University of Arkansas
$292,893
2006–IJ–CX–0026

Terrorism in Time and Space: The Inclusion of Spatio-Temporal Data From Federal Terrorism Cases into the ATS Database
University of Arkansas
$350,000
2006–IJ–CX–0037

Using Data Mining to Identify Patterns in Hostile Surveillance
Research Triangle Institute
$124,919
2006–IJ–CX–0024

Social Science Research on the Role and Impact of Forensic Evidence on the Criminal Justice Process

California State University–Los Angeles
$600,000
2006–DN–BX–0094

Institute for Law and Justice, Inc.
$600,000
2006–DN–BX–0095

Study of Administration of Justice in Indian Country

University of California
$1,472,042
2006–DD–BX–0557

Transnational Crime

Human Trafficking: A Case Study Approach to the Transnational Movement of Chinese Women for Sex Work
Rutgers State University of New Jersey
$284,287
2006–IJ–CX–0008

Prosecuting Human Trafficking Cases: Lessons Learned and Best Practices From the United States and Abroad
Caliber Associates, Inc.
$189,420
2006–IJ–CX–0010

W.E.B. Dubois Fellowship

Significance of Courtroom Workgroup Racial Diversity to Criminal Case Outcomes
Northeastern University
$75,523
2006–IJ–CX–0009

Appendix C
NIJ Publications, Products, and
Web Dissemination in FY 2006

Most NIJ materials are free and can be obtained from these three sources:

• NIJ Web site: www.ojp.usdoj.gov/nij.

• National Criminal Justice Reference Service (NCJRS): www.ncjrs.gov, 800-851-3420, P.O. Box 6000, Rockville, MD 28049-6000.

• National Law Enforcement and Corrections Technology Center (NLECTC) (for science and technology materials): www.justnet.org, 800-248-2742.

Publications (in alphabetical order):

"Automated Information Sharing: Does It Help Law Enforcement Officers Work Better?" *NIJ Journal*, No. 253, January 2006: 25–26.

"Analyzing Terror: Researchers Study the Perpetrators and the Effects of Suicide Terrorism," Hronick, Michael S., *NIJ Journal*, No. 254, July 2006: 8–11.

"Body Armor Safety Initiative: To Protect and Serve . . . Better," Tompkins, Dan, *NIJ Journal*, No. 254, July 2006: 2–6.

Communications Interoperability: Basics for Practitioners, In Short, March 2006, 2 pages, NCJ 212978.

Co-Offending and Patterns of Juvenile Crime, McCord, Joan, and Kevin P. Conway, Research in Brief, December 2005, 20 pages, NCJ 210360.

"Digital Evidence: How Law Enforcement Can Level the Playing Field With Criminals," Ritter, Nancy, *NIJ Journal*, No. 254, July 2006: 20–22.

"DNA Analysis for 'Minor' Crimes: A Major Benefit for Law Enforcement," Zedlewski, Edwin, and Mary B. Murphy, *NIJ Journal*, No. 253, January 2006: 2–5.

Drug Courts: The Second Decade, Special Report, June 2006, 38 pages, NCJ 211081.

Enhancing Police Integrity, Klockars, Carl B., Sanja Kutnjak Ivkovich, and Maria R. Haberfeld, Research for Practice, December 2005, 16 pages, NCJ 209269.

Exploring the Spatial Configuration of Places Related to Homicide Events, Groff, Elizabeth, and Tom McEwen, Final Report, March 2006, 136 pages, NCJ 214254.

Extent, Nature, and Consequences of Rape Victimization: Findings From the National Violence Against Women Survey, Tjaden, Patricia, and Nancy Thoennes, Special Report, January 2006, 46 pages, NCJ 210346.

"Has Rape Reporting Increased Over Time?" Taylor, Lauren R., *NIJ Journal*, No. 254, July 2006: 28–30.

I-SAFE Evaluation, Chibnall, Susan, Madeleine Wallace, Christine Leicht, and Lisa Lunghofer, Final Report, January 2006, 222 pages, NCJ 213715.

Justicia Penal Siglo XXI: Una Selección de Criminal Justice 2000, CD–ROM, August 2006, NCJ 213798.

Juvenile Accountability Incentive Block Grants: Assessing Initial Implementation, Parent, Dale G., and Liz Barnett, Research for Policy, December 2005, 9 pages, NCJ 210116.

"Keeping an Eye on School Security: The Iris Recognition Project in New Jersey Schools," Cohn, Jeffrey P., *NIJ Journal,* No. 254, July 2006: 12–15.

Lessons Learned From 9/11: DNA Identification in Mass Fatality Incidents, September 2006, 142 pages, NCJ 214781.

Lessons Learned From 9/11: DNA Identification in Mass Fatality Incidents, CD–ROM, September 2006, NCJ 215295.

"Maximize Your Evaluation Dollars," Zedlewski, Edwin, and Mary B. Murphy, *NIJ Journal,* No. 254, July 2006: 16–19.

"Methamphetamine Abuse: Challenges for Law Enforcement and Communities," Hunt, Dana E., *NIJ Journal,* No. 254, July 2006: 24–27.

"Police Responses to Officer-Involved Shootings," *NIJ Journal,* No. 253, January 2006: 21–24.

"Predicting a Criminal's Journey to Crime," *NIJ Journal,* No. 253, January 2006: 10–15.

Principles of Forensic DNA for Officers of the Court, President's DNA Initiative, Online Training, February 2006, NCJ 212399.

Public Law 280 and Law Enforcement in Indian Country—Research Priorities, Goldberg, Carole, and Heather Valdez Singleton, Research in Brief, December 2005, 20 pages, NCJ 209839.

Radio Spectrum, In Short, August 2006, 2 pages, NCJ 214962.

Reducing Gun Violence: Community Problem Solving in Atlanta, Kellerman, Arthur L., Dawna Fuqua-Whitley, and Constance S. Parramore, Research Report, June 2006, 40 pages, NCJ 209800.

Sexual Assault on Campus: What Colleges and Universities Are Doing About It, Karjane, Heather M., Bonnie S. Fisher, and Francis T. Cullen, Research for Practice, December 2005, 21 pages, NCJ 205521.

Status and Needs of Forensic Science Service Providers: A Report to Congress, March 2006, 34 pages, NCJ 213420.

Telephony Implications of Voice over Internet Protocol, In Short, February 2006, 2 pages, NCJ 212976.

Test Results for Hardwire Write Block Device: Digital Intelligence Firefly 800 IDE (FireWire Interface), Special Report, April 2006, 18 pages, NCJ 212957.

Test Results for Hardware Write Block Device: Digital Intelligence UltraBlock SATA (FireWire Interface), Special Report, May 2006, 18 pages, NCJ 214067.

Test Results for Hardware Write Block Device: Digital Intelligence UltraBlock SATA (USB Interface), Special Report, April 2006, 19 pages, NCJ 212961.

Test Results for Hardware Write Block Device: FastBloc IDE (Firmware Version 16), Special Report, April 2006, 36 pages, NCJ 212956.

Test Results for Hardware Write Block Device: ICS ImageMasster DriveLock IDE (Firmware Version 17), Special Report, April 2006, 36 pages, NCJ 212959.

Test Results for Hardware Write Block Device: MyKey NoWrite (Firmware Version 1.05), Special Report, April 2006, 28 pages, NCJ 212958.

Test Results for Hardware Write Block Device: WiebeTech Bus Powered Forensic ComboDock (FireWire Interface), Special Report, May 2006, 19 pages, NCJ 214066.

Test Results for Hardware Write Block Device: WiebeTech Bus Powered Forensic ComboDock (USB Interface), Special Report, May 2006, 19 pages, NCJ 214065.

Test Results for Hardware Write Block Device: WiebeTech FireWire DriveDock Combo (FireWire Interface), Special Report, April 2006, 18 pages, NCJ 212960.

Test Results for Hardware Write Block Device: WiebeTech Forensic ComboDock (FireWire Interface), Special Report, May 2006, 18 pages, NCJ 214064.

Test Results for Hardware Write Block Device: WiebeTech Forensic ComboDock (USB Interface), Special Report, May 2006, 19 pages, NCJ 214063.

"Tracking Prisoners in Jail With Biometrics: An Experiment in a Navy Brig," Miles, Christopher A., and Jeffrey P. Cohn, *NIJ Journal,* No. 253, January 2006: 6–9.

"Victim Satisfaction With the Criminal Justice System," *NIJ Journal,* No. 253, January 2006: 16–18.

Visualization of Spatial Relationships in Mobility Research: A Primer, Groff, Elizabeth, and Thomas McEwen, Final Report, March 2006, 65 pages, NCJ 214255.

Exhibit C-1: Top 25 Publications Accessed From the NIJ Web Site, FY 2006

Title and Author	NCJ Number	Published
Crime Scene Investigation: A Guide for Law Enforcement (Research Report), Technical Working Group on Crime Scene Investigation	NCJ 178280	2000
Electronic Crime Scene Investigation: A Guide for First Responders (NIJ Guide), Technical Working Group for Electronic Crime Scene Investigation	NCJ 187736	2001
Convicted by Juries, Exonerated by Science: Case Studies in the Use of DNA Evidence to Establish Innocence After Trial (Research Report), Edward Connors, Thomas Lundregan, Neal Miller, and Tom McEwen	NCJ 161258	1996
Death Investigation: A Guide for the Scene Investigator (Research Report), National Medicolegal Review Panel and Steven C. Clark	NCJ 167568	1999
Guns in America: National Survey on Private Ownership and Use of Firearms (Research in Brief), Philip J. Cook and Jens Ludwig	NCJ 165476	1997
Full Report of the Prevalence, Incidence, and Consequences of Violence Against Women: Findings From the National Violence Against Women Survey (Research Report), Patricia Tjaden and Nancy Thoennes	NCJ 183781	2000
The Sexual Victimization of College Women (Research Report), Bonnie S. Fisher, Francis T. Cullen, and Michael G. Turner	NCJ 182369	2000
What Every Law Enforcement Officer Should Know About DNA Evidence (Research Report), National Commission on the Future of DNA Evidence	BC 000614	1999
2000 Arrestee Drug Abuse Monitoring: Annual Report (Research Report), Arrestee Drug Abuse Monitoring Program	NCJ 193013	2003
Forensic Examination of Digital Evidence: A Guide for Law Enforcement (Special Report), Technical Working Group for the Examination of Digital Evidence	NCJ 199408	2004
Mapping Crime: Understanding Hot Spots (Special Report), John E. Eck, Spencer Chainey, James G. Cameron, Michael Leitner, and Ronald E. Wilson	NCJ 209393	2005
Correctional Boot Camps: A Tough Intermediate Sanction (Research Report), Doris L. MacKenzie and Eugene E. Hebert	NCJ 157639	1996
Extent, Nature, and Consequences of Intimate Partner Violence: Findings From the National Violence Against Women Survey (Research Report), Patricia Tjaden and Nancy Thoennes	NCJ 181867	2000
Sexual Assault on Campus: What Colleges and Universities Are Doing About It (Research for Practice), Heather M. Karjane, Bonnie S. Fisher, and Francis T. Cullen	NCJ 205521	2005
Co-Offending and Patterns of Juvenile Crime (Research in Brief), Joan McCord and Kevin P. Conway	NCJ 210360	2005
Extent, Nature, and Consequences of Rape Victimization: Findings From the National Violence Against Women Survey (Special Report), Patricia Tjaden and Nancy Thoennes	NCJ 210346	2006
Managing Adult Sex Offenders in the Community—A Containment Approach (Research in Brief), Kim English, Suzanne Pullen, and Linda Jones	NCJ 163387	1997
Using DNA to Solve Cold Cases (Special Report), National Commission on the Future of DNA Evidence	NCJ 194197	2002
Police Attitudes Toward Abuse of Authority: Findings From a National Study (Research in Brief), Daniel Weisburd and Rosann Greenspan with Edwin E. Hamilton, Hubert Williams, and Kellie A. Bryant	NCJ 181312	2000
Eyewitness Evidence: A Guide for Law Enforcement (Research Report), Technical Working Group for Eyewitness Evidence	NCJ 178240	1999
Sex Offender Community Notification: Assessing the Impact in Wisconsin (Research in Brief), Richard G. Zevitz and Mary Ann Farkas	NCJ 179992	2000
Child Sexual Molestation: Research Issues (Research Report), Robert A. Prentky, Raymond A. Knight, and Austin F.S. Lee	NCJ 163390	1997
The Appropriate and Effective Use of Security Technologies in U.S. Schools: A Guide for Schools and Law Enforcement Agencies (Research Report), Mary W. Green	NCJ 178265	1999
Enhancing Police Integrity (Research for Practice), Carl B. Klockars, Sanja Kutnjak Ivkovich, and Maria R. Haberfeld	NCJ 209269	2005
"Broken Windows" and Police Discretion (Research Report), George L. Kelling	NCJ 178259	1999

Exhibit C-2: Top 25 Publications by Number of Paper Copies Requested, FY 2006

Title and Author	Quantity	NCJ Number	Published
Principles of Forensic DNA for Officers of the Court (CD–ROM), President's DNA Initiative	6,046	NCJ 212399	2006
Crime Scene Investigation: A Guide for Law Enforcement (Research Report), Technical Working Group on Crime Scene Investigation	3,646	NCJ 178280	2000
Electronic Crime Scene Investigation: A Guide for First Responders (NIJ Guide), Technical Working Group for Electronic Crime Scene Investigation	2,974	NCJ 187736	2001
Death Investigation: A Guide for the Scene Investigator (Research Report), National Medicolegal Review Panel and Steven C. Clark	2,572	NCJ 167568	1997
Eyewitness Evidence: A Guide for Law Enforcement (Research Report), Technical Working Group for Eyewitness Evidence	2,319	NCJ 178240	1999
A Guide for Explosion and Bombing Scene Investigation (Research Report), Technical Working Group for Bombing Scene Investigation	2,154	NCJ 181869	2000
What Every Law Enforcement Officer Should Know About DNA Evidence (Research Report), National Commission on the Future of DNA Evidence	1,811	BC 000614	1999
Identifying Victims Using DNA: A Guide for Families (Brochure), President's DNA Initiative	1,750	NCJ 209493	2005
Mass Fatality Incidents: A Guide for Human Forensic Identification (Special Report), Technical Working Group for Mass Fatality Forensic Identification	1,719	NCJ 199758	2005
Crime Scene Investigation: A Reference for Law Enforcement Training (Special Report), Technical Working Group on Crime Scene Investigation	1,480	NCJ 200160	2004
Fire and Arson Scene Evidence: A Guide for Public Safety Personnel (Research Report), Technical Working Group on Fire/Arson Scene Investigation	1,439	NCJ 181584	2000
DNA in "Minor" Crimes Yields Major Benefits in Public Safety (In Short)	1,213	NCJ 207203	2004
Forensic Examination of Digital Evidence: A Guide for Law Enforcement (Special Report), Technical Working Group for the Examination of Digital Evidence	1,020	NCJ 199408	2004
Lessons Learned From 9/11: DNA Identification in Mass Fatality Incidents (Special Report), President's DNA Initiative	1,014	NCJ 214781	2006
Radio Spectrum (In Short)	1,005	NCJ 214962	2006
Telephony Implications of Voice over Internet Protocol (In Short)	956	NCJ 212976	2006
Using DNA to Solve Cold Cases (Special Report), National Commission on the Future of DNA Evidence	938	NCJ 194197	2002
Education and Training in Forensic Science: A Guide for Forensic Science Laboratories, Educational Institutions, and Students (Special Report), Technical Working Group for Education and Training in Forensic Science	935	NCJ 203099	2004
Mapping Crime: Understanding Hot Spots (Special Report), John E. Eck, Spencer Chainey, James G. Cameron, Michael Leitner, and Ronald E. Wilson	891	NCJ 209393	2005
Co-Offending and Patterns of Juvenile Crime (Research in Brief), Joan McCord and Kevin P. Conway	890	NCJ 210360	2005
Communications Interoperability: Basics for Practitioners (In Short)	801	NCJ 212978	2006
NIJ Journal, Issue No. 252	760	NCJ 208702	2005
NIJ Journal, Issue No. 253	745	NCJ 212261	2006
Drug Courts: The Second Decade (Special Report)	739	NCJ 211081	2006
Advancing Justice Through DNA Technology (Legislation), U.S. Executive Office of the President	735	NCJ 200005	2003

Exhibit C-3: NIJ Web Site Visits, FY 2003–2006

	FY 2003	FY 2004	FY 2005	FY 2006
NIJ Web Site	904,969	1,017,169	1,181,936	1,423,712

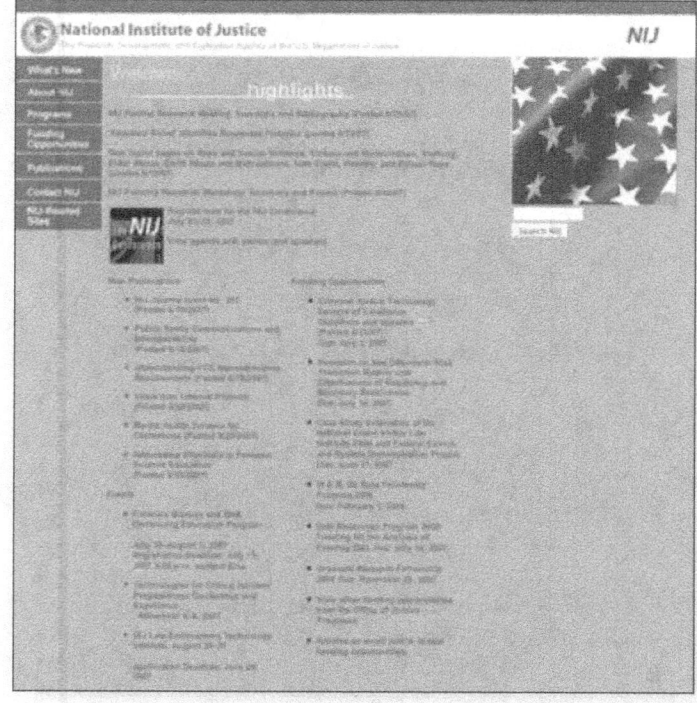

The National Institute of Justice is the research, development, and evaluation agency of the U.S. Department of Justice. NIJ provides objective, independent, evidence-based knowledge and tools to enhance the administration of justice and public safety.

The National Institute of Justice is a component of the Office of Justice Programs, which also includes the Bureau of Justice Assistance; the Bureau of Justice Statistics; the Community Capacity Development Office; the Office for Victims of Crime; the Office of Juvenile Justice and Delinquency Prevention; and the Office of Sex Offender Sentencing, Monitoring, Apprehending, Registering, and Tracking (SMART).

Photo Sources: PunchStock, Jupiter Images, and Picturequest

NCJ 218970

www.ingramcontent.com/pod-product-compliance
Lightning Source LLC
Chambersburg PA
CBHW080519290526
45790CB00006B/2232